S0-BHT-405

Document Delivery Services: Contrasting Views

Document Delivery Services: Contrasting Views has been co-published simultaneously as *The Reference Librarian*, Number 63 1999.

The Reference Librarian Monographic "Separates"

Below is a list of "separates," which in serials librarianship means a special issue simultaneously published as a special journal issue or double-issue and as a "separate" hardbound monograph. (This is a format which we also call a "DocuSerial.")

"Separates" are published because specialized libraries or professionals may wish to purchase a specific thematic issue by itself in a format which can be separately cataloged and shelved, as opposed to purchasing the journal on an on-going basis. Faculty members may also more easily consider a "separate" for classroom adoption.

"Separates" are carefully classified separately with the major book jobbers so that the journal tie-in can be noted on new book order slips to avoid duplicate purchasing.

You may wish to visit Haworth's website at . . .

http://www.haworthpressinc.com

. . . to search our online catalog for complete tables of contents of these separates and related publications.

You may also call 1-800-HAWORTH (outside US/Canada: 607-722-5857), or Fax 1-800-895-0582 (outside US/Canada: 607-771-0012), or e-mail at:

getinfo@haworthpressinc.com

Document Delivery Services: Contrasting Views, edited by Robin Kinder, MLS (No. 63, 1999). *Reviews the planning and process of implementing document delivery in four university libraries–Miami University, University of Colorado at Denver, University of Montana at Missoula, and Purdue University Libraries.*

The Holocaust: Memories, Research, Reference, edited by Robert Hauptman, PhD, and Susan Hubbs Motin, MLS (No. 61/62, 1998). *"A wonderful resource for reference librarians, students, and teachers . . . on how to present this painful, historical event." (Ephraim Kaye, PhD, The International School for Holocaust Studies, Yad Vashem, Jerusalem)*

Electronic Resources: Use and User Behavior, edited by Hemalata Iver, PhD (No. 60, 1998). *Covers electronic resources and their use in libraries, with emphasis on the Internet and the Geographic Information Systems (GIS).*

Philosophies of Reference Service, edited by Celia Hales Mabry (No. 59, 1997). *"Recommended reading for any manager responsible for managing reference services and hiring reference librarians in any type of library." (Charles R. Anderson, MLS, Associate Director for Public Services, King County Library System, Bellevue, Washington)*

Business Reference Services and Sources: How End Users and Librarians Work Together, edited by Katherine M. Shelfer (No. 58, 1997). *"This is an important collection of papers suitable for all business librarians . . . . Highly recommended!" (Lucy Heckman, MLS, MBA, Business and Economics Reference Librarians, St. Johns's University, Jamaica, New York)*

Reference Sources on the Internet: Off the Shelf and onto the Web, edited by Karen R. Diaz (No. 57, 1997). *Surf off the library shelves and onto the Internet and cut your research time in half!*

Reference Services for Archives and Manuscripts, edited by Laura B. Cohen (No. 56, 1997). *"Features stimulating and interesting essays on security in archives, ethics in the archival profession, and electronic records." ("The Year's Best Profession Reading" (1998), Library Journal)*

Career Planning and Job Searching in the Information Age, edited by Elizabeth A. Lorenzen, MLS (No. 55, 1996). *"Offers stimulating background for dealing with the issues of technology and service . . . A reference tool to be looked at often." (The One-Person Library)*

The Roles of Reference Librarians: Today and Tomorrow, Kathleen Low, MLS (No. 54, 1996). *"A great asset to all reference collections . . . Presents important, valuable information for reference librarians as well as other library users." (Library Times International)*

Reference Services for the Unserved, edited by Fay Zipkowitz, MSLS, DA (No. 53, 1996). *"A useful tool in developing strategies to provide services to all patrons." (Science Books & Films)*

Library Instruction Revisited: Bibliographic Instruction Comes of Age, edited by Lyn Elizabeth M. Martin, MLS (No. 51/52, 1995). *"A powerful collection authored by respected practitioners who have stormed the bibliographic instruction (BI) trenches and, luckily for use, have recounted their successes and shortcomings." (The Journal of Academic Librarianship)*

Library Users and Reference Services, edited by Jo Bell Whitlatch, PhD (No. 49/50, 1995). *"Well-planned, balanced, and informative . . . Both new and seasoned professions will find material for service attitude formation and practical advice for the front lines of service." (Anna M. Donnelly, MS, MA, Associate Professor and Reference Librarian, St. John's University Library)*

Social Science Reference Services, edited by Pam Baxter, MLS (No. 48, 1995). *"Offers practical guidance to the reference librarian . . . A valuable source of information about specific literatures within the social sciences and the skills and techniques needed to provide access to those literatures." (Nancy P. O'Brien, MLS, Head, Education and Social Science Library, and Professor of Library Administration, University of Illinois at Urbana-Champaign)*

Reference Services in the Humanities, edited by Judy Reynolds, MLS (No. 47, 1994). *"A well-chosen collection of situations and challenges encountered by reference librarians in the humanities." (College Research Library News)*

Racial and Ethnic Diversity in Academic Libraries: Multicultural Issues, edited by Deborah A. Curry, MLS, MA, Susan Griswold Blandy, MEd, and Lyn Elizabeth M. Martin, MLS (No. 45/46, 1994). *"The useful techniques and attractive strategies presented here will provide the incentive for fellow professionals in academic libraries around the country to go and do likewise in their own institutions." (David Cohen, Adjunct Professor of Library Science, School of Library and Information Science, Queens College; Director, EMIE (Ethnic Materials Information Exchange); Editor, EMIE Bulletin)*

School Library Reference Services in the 90s: Where We Are, Heading, edited by Carol Truett, PhD (No. 44, 1994). *"Unique and valuable to the teacher-librarian as well as students of librarianship . . . . The overall work successfully interweaves the concept of the continuously changing role of the teacher-librarian." (Emergency Librarian)*

Reference Services Planning in the 90s, edited by Gail Z. Eckwright, MLS, and Lori M. Keenan, MLS (No. 43, 1994). *"This monograph is well-researched and definitive, encompassing reference service as practices by library and information scientists . . . it should be required reading for all profession librarian trainees." (Feliciter)*

Librarians on the Internet: Impact on Reference Services, edited by Robin Kinder, MLS (No. 41/42, 1994). *"Succeeds in demonstrating that the Internet is becoming increasingly a challenging but practical and manageable tool in the reference librarian's ever-expanding armory." (Reference Reviews)*

Reference Service Expertise, edited by Bill Katz (No. 40, 1993). *This important volume presents a wealth of practical ideas for improving the art of reference librarianship.*

Modern Library Technology and Reference Services, edited by Samuel T. Huang, MLS, MS (No. 39, 1993). *"This book packs a surprising amount of information into a relatively few number of pages . . . This book will answer many question." (Science Books and Films)*

Assessment and Accountability in Reference Work, edited by Susan Griswold Blandy, Lyn M. Martin, and Mary L. Strife (No. 38, 1992). *"An important collection of well-written, real-world chapters addressing the central questions that surround performance and services in all libraries." (Library Times International)*

The Reference Librarian and implications of Mediation, edited by M. Keith Ewing, MLS, and Robert Hauptman, MLS (No. 37, 1992). *"An excellent and thorough analysis of reference mediation . . . well worth reading by anyone involved in the delivery of reference services."*

(Fred Batt, MLS, Associate University Librarian for Public Services, California State University, Sacramento)

Library Services for Career Planning, Job Searching and Employment Opportunities, edited by Byron Anderson, MA, MLS (No. 36, 1992). *"An interesting book which tells professional libraries how to set up career information centers . . . clearly valuable reading for anyone establishing a career library." (Career Opportunities News)*

In the Spirit of 1992: Access to Western European Libraries and Literature, edited by Mary M. Huston, PhD, and Maureen Pastine, MLS (No. 35, 1992). *"A valuable and practical [collection] which every subject specialists in the field would do well to consult." (Western European Specialists Section Newsletter)*

Access Services: The Convergence of Reference and Technical Services, edited by Gillian M. McCombs, ALA (No. 34, 1992). *"Deserves a wide readership among both technical and public services librarians . . . highly recommended for any librarian interested in how reference and technical services roles may be combined." (Library Resources & Technical Services)*

Opportunities for Reference Services: The Bright Side of Reference Services in the 1990s, edited by Bill Katz (No. 33, 1991). *"A well-deserved look at the brighter side of reference services . . . Should be read by reference librarians and their administrators in all types of libraries." (Library Times International)*

Government Documents and Reference Services, edited by Robin Kinder, MLS (No. 32, 1991). *Discusses access possibilities and policies with regard to government information, covering such important topics as new and impending legislation, information on most frequently used and requested sources, and grant writing.*

The Reference Library User: Problems and Solutions, edited by Bill Katz (No. 31, 1991). *"Valuable information and tangible suggestions that will help us as a profession look critically at our users and decide how they are best served." (Information Technology and Libraries)*

Continuing Education of Reference Librarians, edited by Bill Katz (No. 30/31, 1990). *"Has something for everyone interested in this field . . . Library trainers and library school teachers may well find stimulus in some of the programs outlined here." (Library Association Record)*

Weeding and Maintenance of Reference Collections, edited by Sydney J. Pierce, PhD, MLS (No. 29, 1990). *"This volume may spur you on to planned activity before lack of space dictates 'ad hoc' solutions." (New Library World)*

Serials and Reference Services, edited by Robin Kinder, MLS, and Bill Katz (No. 27/28, 1990). *"The concerns and problems discussed are those of serials and reference librarians everywhere . . . The writing is of a high standard and the book is useful and entertaining . . . This book can be recommended." (Library Association Record)*

Rothstein on Reference: . . . with some help from friends, edited by Bill Katz and Charles Bunge, PhD, MLS (No. 25/26, 1990). *"An important and stimulating collection of essays on reference librarianship . . . Highly recommended!" (Richard W. Grefrath, MA, MLS, Reference Librarian, University of Nevada Library) Dedicated to the work of Sam Rothstein, one of the world's most respected teachers of reference librarians, this special volume features his writings as well as articles written about him and his teachings by other professionals in the field.*

Integrating Library Use Skills into the General Education Curriculum, edited by Maureen Pastine, MLS, and Bill Katz (No. 24, 1989). *"All contributions are written and presented to a high standard with excellent references at the end of each . . . One of the best summaries I have seen on this topic." (Australian Library Review)*

Expert Systems in Reference Services, edited by Christine Roysdon, MLS, and Howard D. White, PhD, MLS (No. 23, 1989). *"The single most comprehensive work on the subject of expert systems in reference service." (Information Processing and Management)*

Information Brokers and Reference Services, edited by Bill Katz, and Robin Kinder, MLS (No. 22, 1989). *"An excellent tool for reference librarians and indispensable for anyone seriously considering their own information-brokering service." (Booklist)*

Information and Referral in Reference Services, edited by Marcia Stucklen Middleton, MLS and Bill Katz (No. 21, 1988). *Investigates a wide variety of situations and models which fall under the umbrella of information and referral.*

Reference Services and Public Policy, edited by Richard Irving, MLS, and Bill Katz (No. 20, 1988). *Looks at the relationship between public policy and information and reports ways in which libraries respond to the need for public policy information.*

Finance, Budget, and Management for Reference Services, edited by Ruth A. Fraley, MLS, MBA, and Bill Katz (No. 19, 1989). *"Interesting and relevant to the current state of financial needs in reference service . . . A must for anyone new to or already working in the reference service area." (Riverina Library Review)*

Current Trends in Information: Research and Theory, edited by Bill Katz, and Robin Kinder, MLS (No. 18, 1984). *"Practical direction to improve reference services and does so in a variety of ways ranging from humorous and clever metaphoric comparisons to systematic and practical methodological descriptions." (American Reference Books Annual)*

International Aspects of Reference and Information Services, edited by Bill Katz, and Ruth A. Fraley, MLS, MBA (No. 17, 1987). *"An informative collection of essays written by eminent librarians, library school staff, and others concerned with the international aspects of information work." (Library Association Record)*

Reference Services Today: From Interview to Burnout, edited by Bill Katz, and Ruth A. Fraley, MLS, MBA (No. 16, 1987). *Authorities present important advice to all reference librarians on the improvement of service and the enhancement of the public image of reference services.*

The Publishing and Review of Reference Sources, edited by Bill Katz, and Robin Kinder, MLS (No. 15, 1987). *"A good review of current reference reviewing and publishing trends in the United States . . . will be of interest to intending reviewers, reference librarians, and students." (Australasian College Libraries)*

Personnel Issues in Reference Services, edited by Bill Katz, and Ruth Fraley, MLS, MBA (No. 14, 1986). *"Chock-full of information that can be applied to most reference settings. Recommended for libraries with active reference departments." (RQ)*

Reference Services in Archives, edited by Lucille Whalen (No. 13, 1986). *"Valuable for the insights it provides on the reference process in archives and as a source of information on the different ways of carrying out that process." (Library and Information Science Annual)*

Conflicts in Reference Services, edited by Bill Katz, and Ruth A. Fraley, MLS, MBA (No. 12, 1985). *This collection examines issues pertinent to the reference department.*

Evaluation of Reference Services, edited by Bill Katz, and Ruth A. Fraley, MLS, MBA (No. 11, 1985). *"A much-needed overview of the present state of the art vis-a-vis reference service evaluation . . . excellent . . . Will appeal to reference professionals and aspiring students." (RQ)*

Library Instruction and Reference Services, edited by Bill Katz, and Ruth A. Fraley, MLS, MBA (No. 10, 1984). *"Well written, clear, and exciting to read. This is an important work recommended for all librarians, particularly those involved in, interested in, or considering bibliographic instruction . . . A milestone in library literature." (RQ)*

Reference Services and Technical Services: Interactions in Library Practice, edited by Gordon Stevenson and Sally Stevenson (No. 9, 1984). *"New ideas and longstanding problems are handled with humor and sensitivity as practical suggestions and new perspectives are suggested by the authors." (Information Retrieval & Library Automation)*

Reference Services for Children and Young Adults, edited by Bill Katz and Ruth A. Fraley, MLS, MBA (No. 7/8, 1983). *"Offers a well-balanced approach to reference service for children and young adults." (RQ)*

Video to Online: Reference Services in the New Technology, edited by Bill Katz and Ruth A. Fraley, MLS, MBA (No. 5/6, 1983). *"A good reference manual to have on hand . . . well-written, concise, provides[s] a wealth of information." (Online)*

Ethics and Reference Services, edited by Bill Katz and Ruth A. Fraley, MLS, MBA (No. 4, 1982). *Library experts discuss the major ethical and legal implications that reference librarians must take into consideration when handling sensitive inquiries about confidential material.*

Reference Services Administration and Management, edited by Bill Katz and Ruth A. Fraley, MLS, MBA (No. 3, 1982). *Librarianship experts discuss the management of the reference function in libraries and information centers, outlining the responsibilities and qualifications of reference heads.*

Reference Services in the 1980s, edited by Bill Katz (No. 1/2, 1982). *Here is a thought-provoking volume on the future of reference services in libraries, with an emphasis on the challenges and needs that have come about as a result of automation.*

Document Delivery Services: Contrasting Views

Robin Kinder
Editor

Document Delivery Services: Contrasting Views has been co-published simultaneously as *The Reference Librarian*, Number 63 1999.

The Haworth Press, Inc.
New York • London • Oxford

Document Delivery Services: Contrasting Views has been co-published simultaneously as *The Reference Librarian*, Number 63 1999.

The Haworth Press, Inc., 10 Alice Street, Binghamton, NY 13904-1580 USA

Cover design by Thomas J. Mayshock Jr.

Library of Congress Cataloging-in-Publication Data

Document delivery services: contrasting views/Robin Kinder, editor.
     p. cm.
    " . . . Co-published simultaneously as the Reference librarian, number 63, 1999."
    Includes bibliographical references and index.
    ISBN 0-7890-0540-9 (alk. paper)
    1. Academic libraries–United States. 2. Document delivery–United States. I. Kinder, Robin. II. Reference librarian.
Z675.U5D56 1999
025.6–dc21
                                             99-18877
                                               CIP

INDEXING & ABSTRACTING

Contributions to this publication are selectively indexed or abstracted in print, electronic, online, or CD-ROM version(s) of the reference tools and information services listed below. This list is current as of the copyright date of this publication. See the end of this section for additional notes.

- *Academic Abstracts/CD-ROM*

- *Academic Search: data base of 2,000 selected academic serials, updated monthly*

- *BUBL Information Service, An Internet-based information Service for the UK higher education community*

- *CNPIEC Reference Guide: Chinese National Directory of Foreign Periodicals*

- *Current Awareness Abstracts of Library & Information Management Literature, ASLIB (UK)*

- *Current Index to Journals in Education*

- *Educational Administration Abstracts (EAA)*

- *IBZ International Bibliography of Periodical Literature*

- *Index to Periodical Articles Related to Law*

- *Information Science Abstracts*

- *Informed Librarian, The*

- *INSPEC*

- *Journal of Academic Librarianship: Guide to Professional Literature, The*

- *Konyvtari Figyelo-Library Review*

(continued)

- *Library & Information Science Abstracts (LISA)*

- *Library and Information Science Annual (LISCA)*

- *Library Literature*

- *MasterFILE: updated database from EBSCO Publishing*

- *Newsletter of Library and Information Services*

- *OT BibSys*

- *Referativnyi Zhurnal (Abstracts Journal of the All-Russian Institute of Scientific and Technical Information)*

- *Sage Public Administration Abstracts (SPAA)*

Special Bibliographic Notes related to special journal issues (separates) and indexing/abstracting:

- indexing/abstracting services in this list will also cover material in any "separate" that is co-published simultaneously with Haworth's special thematic journal issue or DocuSerial. Indexing/abstracting usually covers material at the article/chapter level.
- monographic co-editions are intended for either non-subscribers or libraries which intend to purchase a second copy for their circulating collections.
- monographic co-editions are reported to all jobbers/wholesalers/approval plans. The source journal is listed as the "series" to assist the prevention of duplicate purchasing in the same manner utilized for books-in-series.
- to facilitate user/access services all indexing/abstracting services are encouraged to utilize the co-indexing entry note indicated at the bottom of the first page of each article/chapter/contribution.
- this is intended to assist a library user of any reference tool (whether print, electronic, online, or CD-ROM) to locate the monographic version if the library has purchased this version but not a subscription to the source journal.
- individual articles/chapters in any Haworth publication are also available through the Haworth Document Delivery Service (HDDS).

Document Delivery Services: Contrasting Views

CONTENTS

ABOUT THE EDITOR

Robin Kinder, MLS, is Reference Librarian in the William Allan Neilson Library at Smith College in Northampton, Massachusetts and Adjunct Lecturer in the School for Information Science and Policy at the Universtiy of New York at Albany, teaching introductory and humanities reference sources and services. She acts as a liason to the Office of Minority Affairs, the Women's Studies Committee, and the School for Social Work. Ms. Kinder's professional associations include the American Library Association, the Association of College and Research Libraries, the ACRL/New England Women's Studies Interest Group, and the Pioneer Valley Association for Academic Librarians. She is Associate Editor of *The Reference Librarian* and *The Acquisitions Librarian*, both Haworth Press journals.

Introduction:
Four Views
of Document Delivery Service

Robin Kinder

Before introducing the four articles on document delivery services, a brief tour of the world of document delivery will explain many of the terms and concepts used in the introduction and later articles.

ELEMENTS OF DOCUMENT DELIVERY

Document delivery as a business is generally considered to have emerged in the 1970's, when the introduction of remote databases increased access to information. Special and corporate libraries lacking collections became the primary users of document delivery. Those who could search and verify the document on remote databases, and deliver these for a fee, became known as information brokers. The technological advances in the past 20 years increased the rate of publication, increased access to these publications and created a demand to acquire documents quickly and cheaply. Commercial document delivery began as an entrepreneurial enterprise to address the demands of users with less access to libraries.

When we speak of document delivery today, we move beyond information brokers, entrepreneurs and local suppliers, although these exist and will continue to exist.

Robin Kinder is Reference Librarian, William Allen Neilson Library, Smith College, Northampton, MA 01063.

[Haworth co-indexing entry note]: "Introduction: Four Views of Document Delivery Service." Kinder, Robin. Co-published simultaneously in *The Reference Librarian* (The Haworth Press, Inc.) No. 63, 1999, pp. 1-23; and: *Document Delivery Services: Contrasting Views* (ed: Robin Kinder) The Haworth Press, Inc., 1999, pp. 1-23. Single or multiple copies of this article are available for a fee from The Haworth Document Delivery Service [1-800-342-9678, 9:00 a.m. - 5:00 p.m. (EST). E-mail address: getinfo@haworth.com].

1

FINDING THE LITERATURE

Libraries have developed pilot projects to test the variables in document delivery–speed, turnaround time, quality, reliability, customer support, etc.–and are the primary sources of research done in the area of document delivery. Businesses as a rule do not generally provide in-depth research articles evaluating their document service in any way as critically as their customers have undertaken to evaluate their services and products. The business literature is generally anecdotal or news announcements of various commercial document suppliers, namely, closures, mergers, or the newest technologies. Technology periodicals such as *Online, Computerworld, Information Today and IEEE Computing* are good sources for late breaking news about technologies. Within the library literature, however, extensive documentation exists on the requirements and guidelines for delivering quality document delivery services by commercial suppliers. Document delivery in its simplest form is the delivery of a document to a requestor. In commercial document delivery, this is a large-scale, high-volume business of supplying published documents to end-users.

In terms of searching the literature, it is nearly impossible to eliminate the term interlibrary loan (ILL) or lending without losing many critical articles on commercial document delivery. To eliminate the term means that many relevant titles are lost; to include ILL as a term means the researcher must determine which articles will provide substantial information on document delivery even as they discuss interlibrary lending. It is not wise to retrieve information on document delivery by eliminating substantial and relevant information on ILL operations in libraries.

The authority on both interlibrary loan and document delivery is Mary E. Jackson of the Association of Research Libraries. Her recently published *Measuring the Performance of Interlibrary Loan Operations in North American Research & College Libraries* is the long-awaited survey and study of the delivery options and services offered by libraries. No one considering the document delivery options available to libraries should overlook the issues and direction of document delivery embedded in the discussion of interlibrary loan.

Higginbottham and Bowdoin's provide an interesting and lively review of document delivery in *Access vs. Assets*. A final monograph by Eleanor Mitchell and Sheila Walters, *Document Delivery Services: Issues and Answers*, is critical and necessary reading for understanding the world of document delivery. While it reviews document suppliers from the librarian's perspective, it is also a casebook for anyone needing the basic operational details for implementing document delivery.

A special issue of *Library Trends*, "Resource Sharing in a Changing Environment," published in January 1997 contains articles by librarians and document suppliers. Randall Wayne Marcinko's article in this issue is particularly compelling for the straightforward description of commercial document delivery as a business, from receiving a request to transmitting it to the client. In a lengthy article, he manages to paint a daunting picture of the hurdles document delivery services confront. Before the researcher pursues brief mentions or one-page articles of little substance, however, it would be wiser to concentrate on the monographs and serials noted above. Above all in the literature, there exists sufficient numbers of accounts of document delivery for a librarian to gain a fairly strong impression of vendors from a customer viewpoint. The databases to explore include *Library Literature, Lexis-Nexis, Expanded Academic Index* for citation or full-text articles and *WorldCat* for the most recent monographic titles. There is so much document delivery literature available that the user will have a difficult time limiting the search to retrieve relevant documents. The databases listed above will provide the most recent articles and monographs, and the dynamic nature of document delivery in terms of transmission, delivery of documents and technology make it imperative to review current literature.

Every viable document service maintains a web site where information on services and pricing exist; it is best to know the general elements of a service, saving the difficult questions of delivery, cost and billing for negotiation. The monographs mentioned above, and current articles are critical to gaining an understanding of the industry.

Interlibrary Loan

It is difficult, as noted above, to discuss document delivery without also discussing interlibrary loan, since libraries have historically provided each other with documents, in formats document delivery cannot transmit easily today: books, audio, video. Document delivery today is almost exclusively about delivering only articles, a notable lack in terms of providing comprehensive services. Even when document delivery provides conference reports, proceedings and the like, those businesses are nowhere near to the level of service of traditional interlibrary loan. At the outset, then, commercial document delivery faces a formidable non-profit competitor.

Publishers

Due to the increasing *electronic* transmission of documents, the erroneous generalization exists that everything can be transmitted via the World Wide Web (WWW). But document delivery is only now taking advantage of the WWW and its ability to transfer text, data and graphics. For example, transferring books electronically is daunting. Publishers do not have the economic incentive to invest in digitizing their stock. To date, there isn't enough incentive to invest in digitizing a publisher's print list of titles, although projects are already here for providing entire document sets online, via the Web. That is, publishers are digitizing certain *kinds* of material for access via the web: historical records, reference works, full-text and indexes and abstracting services. This kind of material is either subject specific, set-specific or collection-specific, rather than general or popular electronic text. Publishers first moved into electronic indexes and abstracts, delivering articles from those sources, yet even today provide the bulk of their delivery via U.S. Mail or telefacsimile, rather than digital transmission via the WWW.

For titles that will sell, publishers can risk the cost; for titles wanted by the consumer–general non-fiction, novels, textbooks, scholarly works–the volume is not there for the publishers to invest. Early works are not in digital format and perhaps will never be; converting current titles to electronic formats requires some economic justification over print. The investment in technology with the capacity to scan, store and transmit documents is still a major inhibitor to access, as is the personnel required to undertake such scanning projects.

KINDS OF DOCUMENT DELIVERY

Document delivery exists on a continuum between publishers or libraries and the end user. There are generally considered to be five notable categories of commercial document delivery, based on Higginbotham and Bowdoin, 1993:

- *Document clearinghouses;*
- *Database producers;*

- *Table of contents vendors; (TOC's)*
- *Full text vendors;*
- *Interlibrary Loan*

University Microfilm is known as the document clearinghouse of theses and dissertations, but also of articles, as it is the major provider of serials in microform to libraries. With so many periodical titles in their collection, UMI moved naturally to providing articles to large bibliographic utilities, such as OCLC.

The Institute for Scientific Information (ISI) is an example of a long-standing citation indexer of articles in the humanities, social sciences and sciences. ISI began as one of the earliest document suppliers via their tear sheets, when the article would be torn from the issue and mailed to the requestor. ISI provides documents to bibliographic utilities, libraries, and research and scientific institutes with *The Genuine Article* service. Both services are known as collection-based, as they own the titles requested.

Table of contents vendors are recent arrivals in the industry, but were hatched from the early success of *Current Contents* that gave faculty timely access to information in journals. *CARL Uncover* provides this kind of service, begun with cooperative libraries in Colorado, and now spun into a Knight Ridder subsidiary.

The latest arrival on the full-text scene is OCLC's *Electronic Collections Online* (ECO), containing over 1,000 full text articles to scholarly journals since 1997. A fairly small database, but a strong instance of a library-wise utility providing more than the current popular journal articles and the few full-text scholarly articles currently available in many full-text sources.

PROVIDING BASIC SERVICES TO CLIENTELE

The minimum service libraries now expect from document suppliers is at least:

- *Requesting copyright information from publishers and authors;*
- *Providing reliable service in terms of delivery, including speed and quality of the document;*
- *Providing customer support in verification, invoicing and reporting functions;*
- *Reducing costs and unnecessary surcharges.*

Since document delivery is a service industry, it stands to reason that customer support would inhabit three of the four areas.

A document supplier may have determined the length and breadth of the commercial delivery market, eschewing universal service and choosing more specialized areas for collection, verification, location and delivery. A business may choose to provide documents of a certain nature–scientific articles, technical reports or government reports–while the more universal provider chooses both general and academic materials.

There are advantages in both positions. The universal provider will capture a larger market with easy to deliver articles from accessible sources, but the environment is labor intensive and costly in terms of personnel, volume and technology. The provider who chooses a subject specific area may operate more leanly, with less personnel more focused search parameters. The subject-specific provider is able to provide a wider range of materials, in terms of articles, reports, proceedings, etc. They will also have a smaller world of publishers to negotiate with than the universal provider will have.

TECHNOLOGY

The costliest area, after personnel, will be the technology needed to implement document delivery to start a business. For instance:

- *Telefacsimile machine*
- *Dedicated telephone and Internet lines*
- *Scanner*
- *File Compression software*
- *Laser printer*
- *Personal computers*
- *Photocopiers*

These are only the basic hardware needed to receive, verify, locate and deliver documents in a quickly transforming information environment.

METHODS OF DELIVERY

Methods of delivery are the single most important critical success factor a business must address, since it single-handedly determines customer support and satisfaction.

Mail and Courier

The U.S Postal Service is the slowest of delivery systems, and the cheapest, barring their overnight service. Courier services such as United Parcel Service (UPS) or Federal Express are fast, but the cost to the provider is passed on to the consumer. Both mail and courier services will continue to be used for normal or rush requests.

In June 1998, UPS announced secure Web delivery of documents, particularly its UPS Online Courier service which works with open Internet standards. The Courier service will offer password protection, encryption and tracking and receipt of documents, based on the *Posta 2.0* file attachment application by Tumbleweed Software. The price of transmission is predicted to be significantly lower than overnight delivery service.

Telefacsimile

Telefacsimile is the technology most often used today, and most consumers have access to a fax machine or fax/modem on their personal computers. With sophisticated telefacsimile containing memory for batch delivery during low-peak hours to programmable dialing and automatic document feeders, a provider would profit by eliminating fax surcharge to customers (Higginbotham, 1993). With an Internet line and server, providers can by-pass the costs of telecommunications.

Ariel and DDTP

The latest developments in document delivery have arrived in the dynamic environment of the Web. It is unsurprising that a vehicle for transmitting digitized information would be the next, most desirable step. Digitizing information, however, and transmitting it has emerged only in the last few years with two notable projects: the Research Libraries Group development of Ariel and the North Carolina State University's Document *Delivery Transmission Project (DDTP)*. There are drawbacks to each, and a decision to purchase the hardware and software for Internet transmission is critical.

To deliver documents using *Ariel*, the following components are necessary:

- *File compression software (Ariel)*
- *Scanner*

- *Laser printer*
- *PC to send and receive documents*

Scanning is more reliable than fax, faster and less expensive to use. The use of photocopy or fax cannot match the image quality of scanning, nor deliver the tables, charts, illustrations and other graphic images that are critical to scientists and scholars. The drawbacks are that both the sender and receiver must have *Ariel* software and workstations purchased according to specifications.

The *DDTP* project also employs FTP as the transfer method, but utilizes a Macintosh, printer and scanner. None of the equipment is customized and *DDTP* can transmit across computer platforms, delivering documents into any software package installed (Higginbotham, 1993). The most notable differences in these technologies compared to fax is the speed and quality of the documents and the absence of telecommunications charges since the provider transmits over the Internet.

MIME/ADOBE PDF/ETC

A third option is available to providers: *Multipurpose Internet Mail Extension* or *MIME*. Yem Sui Fong supplies a very succinct look at how MIME works as a document delivery vehicle:

1. *Request enables the user to initiate a request via email to an institution that could fill the request.*
2. *Recording entails the actual process of scanning a document that results in an image file stored on a disk. (cont.)*
3. *Transmission uses Standard MIME compliant e-mail software to transmit the scanned file back to the requester . . .*
4. *Receipt decodes the image file automatically and saves it to disk. A document could then be viewed, printed, saved or forwarded to an individual with MIME compliant mailer or sent to a fax number for printing. (Fong, 1996)*

The advantage in *MIME* is its independent hardware, used with *MIME* compliant mail programs such as Eudora, pine, and Quickmail among many. Portable Document Format (PDF) by Adobe allows viewers to receive documents and transmit to any platform with Adobe residing on it, providing high quality graphic images. Value-added services from mail programs–and file compression software such as *Ariel* and *DTTP*–include technical support, track record, and management reporting functions and electronic notification to clients of document status. Libraries who entertain ideas of entering into fee-based document delivery need to understand these value-added services as competitive forces to be reckoned with, following their examples in terms of both technology and value-added services. While traditional ILL may be well ahead of commercial document delivery in terms of research, verification and location, it must be notably behind in areas of value-added services, primarily due to staffing, rather than the acquisition of hardware or software.

Electronic Transmission: A Few Light Years Away

As a caution to the Internet-driven document supplier, Randall Marcinko notes three reasons why electronic transmission is still an under-utilized area: (1) publications are primarily print, not electronic; (2) scanning paper documents results in high capital and labor costs; and (3) declining telecommunications costs are still higher than shipping of documents by mail or courier (Marcinko, 1997).

Can a company entering the document delivery business compete? Within the past six months, two major document suppliers (*EbscoDoc and UMI's The Information Store*) have closed their document delivery service. Issues providers must contend with are as follows:

- *increasing cost of copyright permission (with Elsevier recently instituting a flat $19 copyright fee for all articles),*
- *high labor costs requiring professional information personnel such as researchers and technical support;*
- *labor-intensive enterprise, involving verification, location, and quality control checks of documents (the latter is reduced with scanning);*
- *capital costs for hardware and software, including management systems for reporting and invoicing*
- *research and development in artificial systems that can handle routine requests. (Marcinko, 1997)*

In a September 14, 1998 letter placed temporarily on the Ebsco Information Services web site, President J. T. Stephens announced the following about the closure of EbscoDoc:

Our decision stems from our sense of industry transition, and a judgement of unacceptable economics. In today's world, a document delivery company faces government-subsidized competition, increasingly costly and restrictive publisher licensing, and the need for significant technical investment with very low cost/revenue margins to provide a return on this investment. *(Stephens, 9/14/98)*

Due to the recent closures of document delivery suppliers, and the low profit margin enjoyed by those who remain, many predict the document supply industry will return to its entrepreneurial foundations. Others maintain that only those suppliers with established reputations will be able to dominate in the industry, large bibliographic utilities such as OCLC and RLIN, or clearinghouses such as UMI and ISI. It is comparable to viewing Bertelsman AG to Graywolf Press, the large publishing conglomerates to the small independent publisher.

In addition, the WWW has developed an electronic publishing industry as well, from electronic journals to reference works to full-text online services. If the most requested documents can be obtained via full-text services such as *Lexis-Nexis, Dow Jones, Infotrac's Expanded Academic and Magazine Indexes, OCLC's Electronic Collections Online* and *EbscoHost*, to name only a few, what will be left to document providers to provide? Presumably, those documents that are most difficult to verify and locate, the precise point where the document supplier begins to lose money.

Most large document suppliers provide a large majority of their requests to bibliographic utilities and libraries. Commercial document delivery cannot easily compete with established traditions among libraries–like interlibrary loan–in terms of research personnel, collections and reciprocal lending and borrowing agreements. Libraries will continue to supplement their own service with a commercial service, but perhaps only for "difficult" documents, or increasingly, to augment their decreased funds for serials acquisitions.

FOUR ARTICLES OF DOCUMENT DELIVERY

This volume reviews the planning and process of implementing document delivery in four libraries–Miami University, University of Colorado at Denver, University of Montana at Missoula and Purdue University Libraries. The major considerations leading to document delivery services were the following: collection development issues, particularly as an alternative access service to canceled serial subscriptions, user needs and expectations, including faculty, students and outside clientele; and the reorganization of the libraries to incorporate enhanced services to the users.

Each article may emphasize a single theme, such as providing document delivery to offset serials cancellations; other issues inevitably appear or are explicitly noted, such as the impact on library staffing, or the impact of the Internet in exponentially increasing avenues of information access. Philosophical questions such as fees or the nature of research lie in the background or are squarely in the foreground in terms of access or ownership. Reading all four articles provides a fairly complete experience of the issues a library will confront in bringing full-service document delivery to its clientele. A number of interesting issues may be examined individually, selected to provide the most critical concerns surrounding document delivery.

COLLECTION DEVELOPMENT

The single most important aspect of implementing document delivery services in a library revolves around the issue of collection development. Even if the library promotes document delivery as information access, the introduction of document delivery impacts on what the library will acquire in the future.

In two articles, collection development is addressed in two different scenarios: as part of a larger effort to create a collection development policy concerning access and ownership, and as part of a service offered in the face of looming serials cancellations. While each article relates an individual library's experience, common themes appear in each: the planning process, implementation of a service and evaluation of either user satisfaction and/or vendor performance.

Auraria Library and Collection Development

The libraries in these articles view collection development as one of the major reasons for testing and implementing document delivery services beyond traditional ILL. Such services emphasize the most appropriate material thus far for commercial delivery–journal literature. The increasing cost of journal subscriptions, the subsequent decline in monograph budgets and shrinking library budgets have pushed libraries to consider access to journal literature as part of collection development.

In Colorado, the Auraria Library undertook a major project to assess the collection and clientele of its three major campuses. The project included reviewing academic departments and degree granting status, student enrollment, graduate programs and areas of faculty research, each weighed in terms of priority collection development. Emphasis is placed on creating a comprehensive collection development policy and philosophy.

Auraria Library undertook the study from concerns about the library's ability to meet the information needs of its clientele based on its in-house collection to examining issues of access or ownership of documents. What will be looked at later, and only noted here, are the presence of general full-text resources such as *EbscoHost, Expanded Academic Index* and *Lexis-Nexis Academic Universe* that fulfill the majority of undergraduate user needs. The library is thus able to meet a large collection development responsibility towards its primary clientele–undergraduates–through general full-text electronic resources, an explicit and remarkably smooth transition from ownership to access. The process of identifying critical users for creating collection development policy is the initial undertaking by any library.

Another element comes into play when libraries seek to define collection areas and responsibilities: participation in consortia or networks of libraries based on various parameters, such as institutional mandates, proximity, and peer institutions. The largest efforts by libraries to share resources have traditionally been through interlibrary loan (ILL) agreements, via bibliographic utilities, networks and reciprocal agreements. The earliest automation successes were developed in ILL due to electronic access to libraries' holdings. The next wave of electronic access via consortia developed with the shared online catalog, either a single catalog shared by a number of institutions or a network providing access to the catalogs of many libraries.

Many libraries today provide electronic requesting and delivery of documents, generally monographs, with a turn-around time much faster than traditional ILL. The move to electronic requests of documents and courier delivery is one of the most positive access developments to appear most recently. Where electronic document delivery has not successfully addressed delivery of substantial monographs, shared catalogs and networks have stepped in and delivered. (The immediate drawback of this successful system of access and delivery via the online catalog is the increase in the number of recalls for other users.) The primary focus of commercial document delivery today consists primarily of providing journal articles and, to a lesser extent, technical reports, organizational publications and international documents.

Libraries operating within consortial or network arrangements have contracted to request articles as well from other libraries. Auraria Library implemented such a relationship with the University of Colorado at Boulder (UCB), at a cost of $5.00 per article to offset UCB's cost to locate and deliver the requested article. Schafer and Thornton note that in its Expedited Delivery Project over 40% of requested articles were delivered by UCB.

Libraries may belong to more than one network, thereby increasing the avenues of both access and delivery and compounding the variables a library must consider in choosing one service over another. What occurs is that a library may have the following elements in providing access to either local or remote collections:

- *Primary and secondary in-house collection*
- *Electronic requests via a shared catalog or network*
- *Traditional ILL for items not owned by the library*
- *Full text resources*
- *Agreement with another library to provide articles*
- *End-user document delivery or mediated document delivery via electronic databases and table-of-contents services*
- *Full-service document delivery*
- *Fee-based services*

The role of collection development resides squarely in the area of a library's permanent collection. One can easily see that the impact of each subsequent step leads toward access rather than ownership. This is precisely where two major themes intersect to illuminate the philosophical underpinnings of a permanent collection versus the aspect of access. The cost and use of materials warrants and then demands that savings in providing access outweigh traditional notions of ownership. Despite that conclusion, libraries undergo psychic adjustments in their ideas of a collection, in identity, and in relations with users, primarily faculty.

Shared catalogs and networks providing for the delivery of documents among libraries resulted in a positive experience for the user. Delivery of articles can provide the same experience, if planned well and presented carefully. When document delivery is viewed as a temporary panacea for serials cancellations, the negative experience of cancellation will outweigh the benefit of article delivery.

Miami University and Serials Cancellations

While most authorities advise separating the two experiences of serials cancellation and document delivery services, such a separation is difficult to achieve in the real world of libraries. The four articles here describe the intense amount of time and energy involved to plan, implement and continuously evaluate document delivery services. Few libraries staff have the necessary time to undertake such projects unless compelling reasons present themselves, generally serials cancellations, where the proportion of library budgets are spent.

Another area where libraries' literally stumbled onto document delivery services lies in the increased access to electronic databases and table-of-contents services, when such services were initially provided as information tools alone, not delivery services. With document delivery services becoming more widely available via the Internet, libraries confronted the issue of collection development and serials reviews as a matter of course. If a library subscribes to a full-text resource that provides general journal articles, should the library continue to subscribe to the print journal?

Additionally, even if libraries' plan and implement document delivery with no plans for cancellations, the adoption of such services will impact on future serials reviews and collection development issues. Once faculty and students are accustomed to rapid, on-demand delivery of articles, the later prospect of serials cancellations may seem less onerous, if only because users grow accustomed to such services.

Whatever approach is taken the impact on collection development is an issue that asserts itself continuously in terms of budgets and funding. At Miami University Libraries, Goode and Mitchell review two pilot projects designed to offset a reduction in the serials budget. The initial project lasted seven months, its duration abbreviated by the project's expansion. Both projects focused on serials in the sciences where subscription increases are most dramatic and burdensome to libraries. Goode and Mitchell outline some of the positive aspects of the project, including increased access to research areas outside the libraries' collection, increased awareness and value of journal articles and introducing users to an electronic information environment. The role of professional staff in providing profiles and monitoring serials was additionally cited as a positive result, as professional staff collaborated with faculty and achieved a greater awareness of faculty research interests.

One of the primary efforts in offsetting cancellations by providing document delivery lies in user relations, particularly faculty. It is difficult to persuade faculty that a serials cancellation is anything but a decline in departmental funding. It is even more difficult to respond to the claims of a permanent collection by faculty who are either generally or fanatically devoted to the library's collection. Few can document the actual value of a document delivery service except for the intangible qualities of time and speed. The library cannot and does not own the document. Yet, in these pilot projects, document delivery resulted in cost savings to libraries, and this must somehow be conveyed to users early and completely. Miami University undertook the process of laying the groundwork for implementing document delivery, using specific departments and eliciting feedback for evaluating the services. The amount of time professional staff will expend in explaining the process alone can't be underestimated, or its importance overestimated. When serials cancellation is a foregone conclusion, it becomes more critical to address the user populations fears and demands.

Within a single institution, the effort is time-consuming and labor-intensive. When multiple institutions become involved in providing document delivery to participating libraries in networks or consortia, the role of libraries in collection development becomes even more critical and daunting. The libraries' professional staff and the faculty not only need to reach agreement, but must reach agreement with other libraries' beset by the same responsibilities to their clientele. Faculty are noted for the responsibility and involvement to varying degrees in a library's collection development, but remain for the most part blind to the pressing concerns of budgets, escalating prices, and little used materials. Faculty select in their research areas primarily, and the gradual view of a department's collection within a library easily appears haphazard or self-absorbed.

Faculty are additionally unaware of the issues libraries face professionally: ethical, contractual, legal, service and user issues lie primarily beyond the immediate interests of faculty. These issues are left for librarians, except when the issues impact on the permanent collection, as they inevitably will. With each library within a network addressing undergraduate needs, faculty research, collection priorities, cancellations and the like, these concerns are compounded in a networked environment. It is difficult to reach agreement within a single institution, much less consensus among numerous institutions. Again, the work lying behind and ahead in collection development needs adequate preparation and presentation, unless the library can afford to recruit professional staff for a pointless exercise in poor public relations, whether one plans in a single or multiple library environment.

ACCESS TO INFORMATION

Access to information generally appears as the reverse of ownership, in an adverse relationship: access vs. ownership. Libraries have attempted to distance themselves from the negative implications of non-ownership, yet the reality is there. A collection is not built or developed with one-time, on-demand document delivery. Recently, however, OCLC's ECO promised something more:

> As a collection of full-text journals, Electronic Collections Online (ECO) is nothing new. ECO's breakthrough is to assemble the other pieces of the puzzle–accessing, archiving, subscribing, and searching–into one integrated package.
>
> OCLC has negotiated greater rights to journals than those typically held by online hosts. ECO-member libraries have permanent rights to journals for which they have paid, even if they cancel their subscriptions. And if ECO itself should discontinue, OCLC will transfer to each library its entire digital collection. This addresses the issues of ownership and archival permanency that other models of online distribution have overlooked. (O'Leary, 1998)

In terms of a well-known provider of access, technical services, reference and ILL services, OCLC has an inside track when it can deliver ownership solutions to librarian's faced with serials cancellation. If OCLC continues to provide a means for the library to insure to a relative degree parts of its collections, the move to access would not feel like such a loss or punishment, even if cancelled journals deserve to be cancelled.

To many minds, access means lower-priority whereas ownership evokes higher priority status, however professional staff endeavor to paint the picture for faculty. The picture changes only over time, by the changing perception of users who are increasingly desirous of access to material and who could care less for its whereabouts.

Internet and Online Databases

Online catalogs and electronic databases became more ubiquitous in libraries in the past ten years; In the past five years, with an increase in full-text sources, table-of-contents services and Internet access, the library user appears more sophisticated, knowledgeable and demanding. The use of the Internet alone has driven the demands of users for citations found in syllabi, bibliographies and publications, and a generation of users accustomed to the Internet has created an environment for services to address their needs.

In the past, indexing and abstracting services provided the user with sufficient information. Their value when compared to full-text or table-of-contents services are consistently under-valued by users today. Reference librarians daily, perhaps hourly, encounter the user who asks for an immediate full-text document, particularly when confronted with the reality of either photocopying from the libraries' collection or requesting ILL delivery.

When users are directed to full-text resources such as Lexis-Nexis or EbscoHost, the perception is that it is the Internet with the 'answer' rather than a subscription-based resource paid for by the library. The conclusion by the user is that the article was found on the Internet free. The issue of access vs. ownership is meaningless to the user. The ability to define "free" vs. "subscription" isn't the user's task. With the user's perception in mind, libraries attempt to provide a seamless integration of electronic resources. In term of access, libraries are responsible for creating a user-friendly environment, understanding at the same time the problems inherent in creating the environment, notably the user's inability to understand the distinctions in services provided. While faculty are most amenable to normal delivery of materials, the student lies on the continuum between real need and procrastination, generally demanding materials quickly and easily. The user generally does not understand, for instance, the reason a library may provide electronic ordering of monographs from another library, but not journal articles.

The increase in informational resources, particularly the Internet rather than subscription databases, has created a world of users with obscure, incomplete, erroneous or genuinely accurate but unobtainable document requests. To the user, a citation on the Internet proves the existence of a desired document; reference services and ILL absorb the impact of verifying and locating the document, often at the expense of great time and effort. There is, on the other hand, the concomitant use of the Internet by the same staff when searching databases and bibliographic utilities fail to locate the cited document. It is generally agreed that as the Internet has increased the expectations and demands of the user, the Internet has also served as the place where a citation may be located when all else has failed.

Purdue University's Fee-Based Service

Suzanne M. Ward and Mary Dugan provide a fee-based model for creating a research and delivery service within a library. At Purdue University, the initial step into fee-based services sought to address the information needs of Indiana manufacturers, now expanded to include national and global customers. The service is designed on a cost-recovery basis. While some services do realize a profit, the reality of commercial document delivery services operating within a low profit margin makes that realization difficult at best for non-profit institutions. It is not unusual for major university or local college libraries within states or jurisdictions to provide such services to a broader constituency, whether that be a state institution providing services to state residents, or a local college providing services to the local community. As long as the affiliated, priority users are being served, extension of services to outside users depends upon the individual library's service philosophy.

Ward and Dugan succinctly outlines the advantages and disadvantages of incorporating fee-based services, essentially an outsourced research and delivery service within the library. The fee-based service incorporates professional staff to locate and deliver "difficult" documents requested by users, eliminating all but routine requests generally handled by ILL. The fee-based service contains all the elements of a commercial document delivery service, including skilled research staff, contracts with numerous national and international vendors, the technology to receive and deliver documents, and value-added services such as status reports and invoice statements. With such a service in place by the library for outside users, the step toward providing one's own library with the service is fairly evident. The authors also outline the ethical issues libraries must address in incorporating fee-based services and the limitations that libraries must place on fee-based services in terms of the affiliated user.

Online Database Selection and Acquisition

The problem of defining the collection in terms of access means defining the collection in terms of ownership. Librarians cannot easily subscribe to a database without encountering a number of collection development decisions. The primary decision will inevitably be the cancellation of specific titles or indexes duplicated in full-text or document delivery service, such as a table-of-contents service. The proliferation of electronic full-text services and electronic resources caught many libraries by surprise. It would not be unusual for libraries to subscribe to a number of full-text resources that duplicate each others' titles, much less duplicating the library's print and electronic journal collection. Due to the time and effort required in an effort to reduce duplication of titles accessed in local or remote collections, many libraries simply provide the electronic resources, with titles tagged to the library's own collection.

The issues of access and ownership evolve slowly into more comprehensive views of the collection enjoyed by a library. The question of "what will this library acquire?" is also evolutionary, but this has always been so, as faculty arrive and depart, research interests wax and wane, or programs are added or subtracted to the equation. The introduction of electronic access to information has only increased the demand on collections from local and remote users. While access gives the library some breathing room to explore collection development issues, access can also create the need for collection development at warp speed. At times access simply proves to be faster than protracted collection development initiatives. In many cases, such collection development projects are undertaken after the library has overburdened the collection with access to electronic resources.

Libraries need to acquire electronic databases with stringent criteria for inclusion, rather than a general grab bag of offerings. Most libraries do acquire electronic indexing and abstracting services based on curricular and scholarly needs. These services provide the access points to journal and monograph literature that general electronic resources cannot. The level of subject and abstract indexing identifies these sources as information resources. The levels of indexing in full-text and table-of-contents services identify these services as delivery services. Librarians cannot complain, although they often do, about the lack of indexing in table of contents services, simply because the goal of full text or table of contents resources is currency and delivery. Before librarians can accurately judge the merits of electronic resources, it is important that they understand the purpose of the resource, the reality that resources are not created equally and were not meant to be created equally.

Indexing and abstracting services, citation databases, full-text sources, electronic publishing and the Internet have impacted reference services profoundly. Many libraries easily contain 100 databases for their general clientele, with singular and often startling interfaces, search engines and delivery options. In the midst of defining or maintaining traditional areas of collection development in a library, staff in reference must approach electronic collection development with an eye always on the permanent collection. That this is an exhaustive enterprise is hardly surprising. Librarians suffer the most from information overload, combined with an acute sixth sense denied to the average user for selecting and evaluating information. In the area of collection development, the librarian must not only look to the user's needs, but also to the unarticulated and unanticipated needs that electronic resources present to librarians. For the most part, libraries presently add databases with and without much thought, making quick decisions without critically evaluating content, interface, or search capabilities. The result is likely to impact their own work, so it remains to be seen when librarians begin declining sources simply because an interface is notably hideous.

REORGANIZATION

In discussing the impact access has had on reference services, whether from full-text delivery or commercial document delivery from electronic services, this discussion turns to the last theme evident in the articles on document delivery–the implicit or explicit reorganization of a library's services or functions before, during or after implementing document delivery. While "after" may appear to be a late or ill-considered reorganization, a library may simply be unable to anticipate how services and functions will be affected by document delivery services. Some service areas may be altered slightly after the initial review of document delivery services; others may be overhauled overnight in order to achieve a properly functioning service.

How a service may be affected is determined in large part by how the library's administration wants to present their case for the services. When a library presents a case for document delivery in terms of collection development, the movement into and impact on acquisitions services and serials departments is a fairly guaranteed event. Document delivery is viewed as a collection tool to augment the collection, and may be supervised by subject specialists or bibliographers in acquisitions.

Where document delivery is being presented as a supplement to existing delivery services–ILL and courier delivery–the impact of such a service will fall in at least capable, if not over-worked, hands. The major question in supplying document delivery via the ILL services in a library is the extent to which support staff are expected to learn and use document delivery systems. The support staff would need to incorporate a major service into their own services. Even with a librarian overseeing such a move, it is difficult to imagine a supervisor not taking into account this demand for greater skills and expertise from support staff. Support staff are otherwise well-versed in the receipt and delivery of documents, statistical reporting and database searching, primary elements in commercial delivery services as well. Electronic document delivery would require ever more electronic skills, in positions where the work is demanding and labor intensive as is.

The impact of electronic access on public services was mentioned earlier. Placing document delivery services within reference appears to be in line with the requirement of skilled researchers in commercial document delivery. Implementing document delivery as a part of reference services appears to be a least desired method, possibly due to the demands on reference staff and the lack of consistent staffing hour by hour in reference to oversee document delivery. In ILL or acquisitions, it is possible that existing staff could oversee the operation, due to familiarity with either delivery or ownership.

Sue Samson describes the projects of the Mansfield Library at the University of Montana, designed to provide models for information retrieval, collection development and serials access. The difference in these projects is the incorporation of document delivery into ready reference and mediated service by reference staff to undergraduates requesting ILL. Due to the assistance of reference staff in the mediated setting, periodical requests by undergraduates declined. Either reference personnel located the article through the collection or a full text resource, or reference staff were able to direct the undergraduate to equally relevant sources and documents. The mediated environment in terms of assisting in ILL and document delivery services gives the reference staff an opportunity to work with undergraduates on their assignments.

The impact document delivery has on reference services is often either not identifiable or quantifiable, due to the intangible elements in much of what reference librarians' do. Alongside such areas as desk services, instruction, liaison responsibilities, and collection development, additional impacts from document delivery will be hard to perceive as well. Generally speaking, however, a mediated environment will require intervention whereas an unmediated environment will still hold hidden impacts on service. Despite the difference, it is naïve to believe that reference services–public services–will remain unaffected by an electronic service that is tied to the research and collection needs of our clientele, wherever that service is located. Indeed, it would seem difficult to say precisely what service would remain unaffected by the move to document delivery to end user, since it is a complex, dynamic and constantly shifting enterprise.

REFERENCES

Baker, Shirley and Mary E. Jackson. *Maximizing Access, Minimizing Cost: A First Step Toward the Information Access Future.* Washington, DC: ARL Committee on Access to Information Resources, December 1994. <www.arl.org/access/illdd-res/articles/white.paper.html>

Boss, Richard W. and Judy McQueen. *Document Delivery in the United States: a report to the Council on Library Resources.* Washington, DC: Council on Library Resources, 1983.

Chang, Amy and Mary E. Jackson. *Managing Resource Sharing in the Electronic Age.* New York: AMS Press, 1996.

Computers in Libraries (Special Section: Document Delivery) 14:9 (October 1994).

Higginbotham, Barbra Buckner and Sally Bowdoin. *Access vs. Assets.* Chicago: ALA, 1993.

Jackson, Mary E. and Karen Croneis. *Uses of Document Delivery Services.* Washington, DC: Association of Research Libraries, 1994.

Jackson, Mary E. "Document Delivery over the Internet," *Online*, 17:2 (March 1993), 14.

Machlis, Sharon. "UPS Offers Online Delivery," *Computerworld*, 32:25 (June 1998), 10.

Kingma, Bruce. "Interlibrary Loan and Resource Sharing: the Economics of the SUNY Express Consortium; University Libraries of the State University of New York at Albany, Binghamton, Buffalo and Stony Brook," *Library Trends*, 45:3 (January 1997), 518.

Kohl, David. "Revealing UnCover: Simple, Easy Article Delivery," *Online*, 19:3 (May-June 1995) 52.

Marcinko, Randall Wayne. "Issues in Commercial Document Delivery" *Library Trends*, 45:3 (January 1997), 531.

Mitchell, Eleanor and Sheila A. Walters. *Document Delivery Services: Issues and Answers*. Medford, NJ: Learned Information, Inc., 1995.

O'Leary, Mick. "Electronic Collections Online Look Beyond Print," Information Today, 15;9, October, 1998.

Perry, Samuel. "Internet Offers Promise for Secure Document Delivery," *Reuter Business Report*, June 9, 1997.

Tumbleweed Software. "Tumbleweed Software Introduces Posta 2.0: First Comprehensive Platform for Buildings Global Online Delivery Solutions," Redwood City, CA. August 10, 1998. *<www.tumbleweed.com/press/twpres38.htm.>*

Ward, Suzanne. "Document Delivery: Evaluating the Options," *Computers in Libraries*, 17:9 (October 1997), 26.

From Ownership to Access:
Re-Engineering Library Services

Jay Schafer
Glenda A. Thornton

SUMMARY. In 1992, Auraria Library fully embraced the idea that meeting user information needs is a collection development activity which should be funded from the materials budget whether accomplished by purchasing material for permanent retention or by acquiring one-time access for an individual user. This article discusses the restructuring of a traditional Interlibrary Loan Department into Information Delivery/Interlibrary Loan (ID/ILL) and its move to Collection Development Services. Because access to resources was funded from the learning materials budget along with ownership, it became necessary to rethink the Library's collection development philosophy. Implementation of the new philosophy required modification of collection building practices and the creation of aggressive information delivery programs. *[Article copies available for a fee from The Haworth Document Delivery Service: 1-800-342-9678. E-mail address: getinfo@haworthpressinc.com]*

INTRODUCTION

At its December 1993 administrative retreat, the Auraria Library renamed its interlibrary loan operation Information Delivery/Interli-

Jay Schafer is Coordinator of Collection Development Services, Auraria Library, University of Colorado at Denver, 1100 Lawrence Street, Denver, CO 80204 (E-mail: jschafer@carbon.cudenver.edu). Glenda A. Thornton is Associate Director for Library Services, Auraria Library, University of Colorado at Denver, 1100 Lawrence Street, Denver, CO 80204 (E-mail: gthornton@castle.cudenver. edu).

[Haworth co-indexing entry note]: "From Ownership to Access: Re-Engineering Library Services." Schafer, Jay, and Glenda A. Thornton. Co-published simultaneously in *The Reference Librarian* (The Haworth Press, Inc.) No. 63, 1999, pp. 25-40; and: *Document Delivery Services: Contrasting Views* (ed: Robin Kinder) The Haworth Press, Inc., 1999, pp. 25-40. Single or multiple copies of this article are available for a fee from The Haworth Document Delivery Service [1-800-342-9678, 9:00 a.m. - 5:00 p.m. (EST). E-mail address: getinfo@haworthpressinc.com].

brary Loan (ID/ILL), moved it administratively from Serial Services (where it had been temporarily aligned) to Collection Development Services, determined that a full-time, permanent librarian would be hired to expand the operation beyond traditional interlibrary loan activities, and planned a new physical location to increase space and efficiency. More importantly, the Library embraced the concept that meeting user information needs is a collection development activity and should be funded from the materials budget whether accomplished by purchasing material for permanent retention or by acquiring one-time access for an individual user. However, the funding of access to information from the materials budget was not to be accomplished in a vacuum separate from the development of the permanent collection. The Coordinator of Collection Development Services was charged with developing a collection philosophy to establish the guidelines for determining which information sources are cost-effective to add permanently and which are cost-effective to provide on-demand for one time needs.

CHARACTERISTICS OF THE AURARIA LIBRARY

The Auraria Library was established in 1976 as part of the new Auraria Campus in downtown Denver. Serving as home to the Community College of Denver (CCD), Metropolitan State College of Denver (MSCD), and the University of Colorado at Denver (UCD), it is the largest campus of higher education in Colorado. Auraria Library, formed by merging the existing libraries from the three institutions, serves approximately 1,700 faculty and 33,000 head count students, or 23,000 full-time equivalent (FTE) students. In addition, the Library receives about ten percent of its use from local residents.

To provide 87.5 hours of service each week, the Library depends on a staff of 27 library faculty, 61 paraprofessionals, and approximately 16.5 student FTE. The collection consists of approximately 984,000 items, including government publications and a relatively large microforms collection. The total Library budget was $5.4 million in 1995/96, with $1.4 million allocated to learning materials of all types.

There are more postsecondary degrees and certificate degree programs offered on the Auraria campus than any other in Colorado. This includes 117 certificate and associate degree programs, 86 bachelor degree programs, 44 master degree programs, and five doctoral degree programs.[1] Thus, the demands on the Library's learning materials budget and the resulting collection are prodigious.

In the most recent IPEDS (Integrated Postsecondary Education Data System) data (1994),[2] the per FTE student contributions to the Auraria Library by the three academic institutions were:

Community College of Denver	$96
Metropolitan State College of Denver	$198
University of Colorado at Denver	$321
Average for all FTE students at Auraria	$190

This level of financial support is the lowest of any four-year state-supported college or university in Colorado. As a result of the limited financial resources, Auraria Library has the least staffing (librarians and support staff), volumes, and serials per 1,000 FTE students of any four-year, state-supported college or university in Colorado.[3]

THE IMPETUS TO INCORPORATE ACCESS INTO COLLECTION DEVELOPMENT

It is obvious that satisfying the information needs of this large and diverse user population with such limited financial resources is a great challenge. In 1991, Auraria Library initiated a strategic planning process which designated collection development as its number one priority. This emphasis provided visibility and support for collection–building never before known at Auraria. A corps of bibliographers was created whose primary responsibility was collection development.[4] Major accomplishments have been achieved, including greater communication with faculty and weeding of the entire collection. With the development of the Collection Philosophy, greater attention has also been paid to selection with emphasis on achieving maximum cost-effectiveness.

While these changes were being made in collection development, interlibrary loan operations began to receive renewed attention both locally and nationally. In the late 1980s it became clear to the Auraria Library's administration that the Library's interlibrary loan operation left much to be desired. Changes were made to improve the workflow and productivity of the staff. By the early 1990s, there was a demand to find ways to go beyond traditional interlibrary loan services.

STUDY COMMISSIONED AND TASK FORCE APPOINTED

The growing demands on the Auraria Library's ILL operation were not unique within Colorado. Auraria Library reports administratively to the University of Colorado at Denver (UCD), and is a part of the four-campus University of Colorado (CU) system which includes the Boulder campus (UCB), the Colorado Springs campus (UCCS), and the Health Sciences Center (UCHSC), also located in Denver. To determine if there was a more efficient manner of identifying and moving library materials among the four campuses, the CU system library deans and directors commissioned a study of interlibrary loan practices in the summer of 1992. The study recommended that the four campuses establish document delivery services directly with each other, outside of ILL, to improve turnaround times.[5]

A task force was subsequently appointed by the CU system deans and directors to study the feasibility of implementing a direct document delivery service among the four campuses. This task force found that the information needs of the four campuses were so different that, while the speed of delivery could indeed be dramatically improved, such a system would actually have a negative impact upon those campuses which depended heavily upon information providers outside of the CU system and the state. Therefore, the concept of implementing an improved document delivery system among the four CU campuses was abandoned.[6]

However, for the Auraria Library, two important concepts emerged from this early attempt to improve cost-effective access to information not available in the collection. First, it was obvious that the information needs of the four CU campuses could not be satisfied solely from internal resources. This realization led to another system-wide study of the benefits of using commercial document suppliers.

The results of this study were also mixed. The campus with the most learning resources, UCB, felt that the benefits of using commercial document suppliers for its information needs were somewhat limited. On the other hand, Auraria, with a smaller number of resources and a large student body, found the services of commercial document suppliers to be both timely and cost-effective.[7] Thus, by 1994, the use of commercial document suppliers was incorporated as a standard method of supplying information needs at the Auraria Library and was funded from the materials budget.

The second important concept for Auraria was that while UCB could provide a significant portion of Auraria's information needs, the reverse was not true. Although part of the same system, and certainly willing to help, the UCB Libraries found that a commitment to supplying all possible information needs of the Auraria Library would have a negative impact on its staffing and lending operation. Still, with the UCB Libraries only about 40 miles from the Auraria Library, the concept of greater access to UCB's resources was too tantalizing to abandon.

A review of the literature revealed two projects in which libraries had gained improved access to other library collections. Dusenbury describes a project at California State University, Chico, where the Meriam Library subscribed to the research library collection at the University of California, Berkeley, by paying for the additional staff, equipment, and other costs for Berkeley to supply Chico with documents beyond the quantity traditionally supplied by ILL. This resulted in an average cost per article of $10.16; the cost would have been only $5.00 per article had Chico requested the full 1,300 articles that they originally estimated they would need. The median turnaround was three days.[8]

Libraries at James Madison University, Virginia Polytechnic Institute and State University, and the University of Virginia established the Document Express program among themselves to provide 48-hour delivery of articles from a list of over 400 journal titles. The average cost of these articles was $12.68 during the start-up year and was expected to fall to $7.88 for the second year. This compared very favorably to the estimated $20.00 per article cost of obtaining articles on a rush basis from commercial suppliers.[9]

AURARIA-CU BOULDER LIBRARIES EXPEDITED ARTICLE DELIVERY PROJECT

Using the projects described above as models, the Auraria-CU Boulder Libraries Expedited Article Delivery Project was begun in early 1994. This project allows Auraria Library to request all journal articles from the UCB Libraries that they can supply–about 43 percent of Auraria's total requests. For each article, Auraria Library pays $5.00 to offset the cost of the additional staffing required to process a workload which is considerably larger than ordinarily generated by following approved ILL practice. In return, UCB guarantees 48 hour handling, with articles being mailed or faxed directly to the user when requested. This project is also funded directly from the materials budget.

AURARIA LIBRARY COLLECTION PHILOSOPHY

By the December 1993 Auraria Library administrative retreat, much of the groundwork was already laid for the physical and philosophical move of Information Delivery/Interlibrary Loan to Collection Development Services. The two most challenging pieces left to complete were the creation of a written collection philosophy and its introduction to the campus community.

The underlying premise of the philosophy was to satisfy the greatest number of users possible through collection building, while developing an aggressive document delivery program (including traditional ILL) for those materials which are not cost-effective purchases. It was also assumed, rightly as it turned out, that the acquisition of materials for the permanent collection would have to be adjusted to achieve greater cost-effectiveness. Conversely, the Auraria Library did not want to purchase only one time access to information that would be more cost-effective to own permanently.

COST-EFFECTIVENESS OF OWNERSHIP VERSUS ACCESS

The concept of building library collections based on whether it is more economical to own a specific item (depending on anticipated level of usage) or to access it upon demand is relatively new in librarianship and certainly has its detractors. This concept, however, is well grounded in the view of collection building as a science based upon bibliometrics. It seems to be well accepted within the profession that there are patterns to the use of library materials, yet no effective method has been found to use an understanding of these patterns to select materials that will be heavily used or economical to own.

There is as yet no "industry standard" for what constitutes a cost-effective purchase of information, whether intended for ownership or one time use. Although the literature demonstrates an increasing interest in use studies, there are few recently published studies reporting specific circulation use of library materials. In 1992, the University of Tennessee found that the average circulation for a selected group of 8,000 book titles from large LC classes was 26 circulations per title over an eight-year period, while the average circulation of all titles during that period was 2.65.[10] At the Auraria Library it was found that a selected group of 708 book titles circulated 5.7 times each over a five-year period.[11] Charles Hamaker reports that 43 percent of newly acquired and cataloged titles circulated at least once during the first six months of ownership at Louisiana State University.[12]

There is a growing body of literature comparing the cost-effectiveness of journal ownership and interlibrary loans of journal articles to document delivery services. These studies have been stimulated, at least in part, by the publication in 1993 of the *ARL/RLG Interlibrary Loan Cost Study*. Librarians now have a benchmark to use in comparing both the cost and the cost-effectiveness of a variety of means of providing for user information needs. We now know that it costs $18.62, on average, for a research library to borrow an item or receive a photocopy, and $10.93 for another library to lend or supply that item, resulting in a total cost of $29.55 for each completed ILL transaction.[13]

A number of libraries have been using this information to review journal subscriptions and offer subsidized document delivery services in lieu of journal ownership. Gossen and Irving[14] provide the most aggressive study yet of the cost-effectiveness of journal ownership, usage, and the alternative cost of access. They conclude that low-usage periodicals, even when low-cost, are more cost-effective to access than to own.

ELEMENTS IN THE DESIGN
OF THE COLLECTION PHILOSOPHY

Since no one has yet found a way to predict which materials will be used prior to purchase (except for a narrow range of specifically requested materials), Auraria Library has approached the challenge of improving the cost-effectiveness of purchases from another perspective. We have identified those programs which have the greatest number of students, assuming that the materials needed to meet the information needs of these students also have the greatest potential to be used, and used heavily.

Of the 24,238 FTE students on the Auraria campus, approximately 22,006 or 90.8% are undergraduates. Building a core collection of books, journals, electronic, and non-print materials that provides these students with a successful library experience is the major priority of the Collection Philosophy. This strategy is not only statistically motivated. The cost of undergraduate materials is significantly less, allowing more, and more heavily used, material to be purchased.

Two areas of graduate study at UCD have been designated as unique offerings in Colorado state-supported higher education: architecture and public affairs. The Auraria Library has the major responsibility in Colorado for collecting information resources to support these two academic programs as well as to support the state-wide information needs in these two areas. By adding the 478 FTE students enrolled in these two programs to the undergraduate FTE students, the information needs of approximately 92.8% of the student body are being addressed.

Of the 2,233 FTE students enrolled in graduate programs at UCD in 1992/93, approximately 29% were in the School of Business and 33% were in the School of Education. In addition, both of these disciplines have large undergraduate enrollments on campus. Of lesser concern, but still important to an urban academic library, there are large numbers of practitioners and alumni in the area using these materials.

By designating undergraduate programs and the UCD graduate programs of architecture, public affairs, business, and education as the primary collecting priorities of the Auraria Library, the information needs of approximately 98% of the FTE students are being addressed by ownership of materials when possible. It is also within these five categories that all known accreditation of specific programs occurs. The remaining two percent of the FTE student population is made up of UCD graduate enrollment in approximately 26 areas in the College of Liberal Arts & Sciences and at least four areas in the College of Engineering and Applied Science. It is unrealistic, within the fiscal limitations previously described, to believe that the Library can purchase adequate numbers of books and journals to support this two percent of the enrollment and the associated faculty research needs, or that it is cost-effective to do so, given the small number of users and the unlikelihood that these materials would see multiple uses.

IMPLICATIONS OF THE COLLECTION PHILOSOPHY

The implications of the Collection Philosophy to collection building at the Auraria Library were significant. To support the information needs of the undergraduate students, the Library subscribed to the electronic *Expanded Academic Index* and to almost all of the journals it indexed. This provides a broad-based, core collection which satisfies the majority of undergraduate curricular information needs in the humanities, social sciences, and general sciences. The Philosophy also supports the need for a strong book collection at the undergraduate level. For the four supported graduate programs, the collection philosophy calls for purchasing, to the extent fiscally possible, books, journals, and non-print materials that support graduate research. Extensive support of faculty research in these four areas is not a priority. To support the curricular information needs in all remaining areas of graduate study and for much faculty research, Auraria Library is committed to funding information delivery programs from the materials budget. These programs are anticipated to cost up to $100,000 by the year 2000.

Funding the collection needs for the undergraduate programs, four graduate programs, and information delivery programs at an adequate level required a major re-prioritization of the materials budget allocation. Each of the twenty-some smaller graduate programs had previously enjoyed some level of collection-building support. Thus, over $120,000 worth of journal subscriptions were identified in these disciplines as no longer appropriate for purchase. Implementation of the Collection Philosophy required that this money be re-allocated to higher priority areas with greater anticipated use. Conversely, because the materials supporting these programs probably did not receive heavy multiple use, it would be cost-effective to obtain access to this material upon demand.

RATIFICATION OF THE COLLECTION PHILOSOPHY

To gain campus support for the Collection Philosophy, a series of meetings was held with the various campus constituencies. The first of these was with the UCD Vice Chancellor for Academic Affairs and the UCD academic deans. Since all graduate programs on the Auraria campus are located at UCD, these were the administrators most likely to be affected by the Philosophy and the ones most likely to face complaints by unhappy faculty when the implementation (journal cancellations) began. After attending presentations that clearly demonstrated the demographics of student enrollment and the level of fiscal support given the Auraria Library as compared to other libraries in Colorado higher education, the Vice Chancellor and Deans agreed to support the Collection Philosophy and its implementation. Support from the chief academic officers and deans of the other two institutions on campus was easily obtained since they offer only undergraduate programs. Similarly, the Library Advisory Committee (made up of faculty and student representatives of the three institutions) voted unanimously to support the Philosophy and its implementation.

The next step was to take the Philosophy to the campus faculty. Demographic and budget presentations were made at three campuswide faculty meetings. The greatest attendance and most comment came from UCD faculty in those disciplines where journal cancellations were imminent. Even though many did not support the end result, none could fault the rationale of the Philosophy. Anticipating reactions from the UCD applied mathematics and chemistry faculty, the Coordinator for Collection Development and the science bibliographer attended department faculty meetings to explain the Philosophy. Again, the journal cancellations were not a popular idea, but these faculties appreciated the Library's attempt to provide a thoughtful plan of collection building and were intrigued by the possibilities of information delivery.

IMPLEMENTATION OF THE COLLECTION PHILOSOPHY

After the Collection Philosophy was ratified as the guide to collection building at the Auraria Library, a journal review was begun. The Coordinator and bibliographers developed a process to identify those journals that fell outside the parameters defined by the Philosophy. A list of these titles was sent to all campus faculty twice, along with a form to be completed and returned if a faculty member believed a title or titles should be retained. The form requested information regarding the use of the title: undergraduate curriculum use, graduate curriculum use, undergraduate supplemental use, graduate supplemental use, direct support of faculty research, supplemental support of faculty research, and other uses.

The initial cancellation list included 263 titles (9.6% of the subscription base) at a cost of $141,379 (32% of the subscription base cost). Faculty returned comment sheets on 103 titles (costing $60,689). It was determined that 20 titles (costing $15,633) were indeed within the scope of the Philosophy and were retained. Another 49 titles (costing $22,599) received enough justification that the Library is going to retain them while gathering further statistical information on their use. A total of 194 titles (7.1% of the subscription base) costing $103,147 (23% of the subscription base cost) were canceled in 1996.

Most faculty comments were very supportive of the process. A chemistry faculty member wrote "I think your way of doing this is fine. I am sure you will have to stand some criticism, but you have given people the opportunity to comment and you have made some quite rational choices. That is what we pay you top-flight administrators to do!" From a physics professor: "Thank you for the thorough response to my recommendation for your journal review process. I know this is a difficult job, and I appreciate your consideration of the needs of our program." From a business faculty: "You . . . are commended on the fine results of the process! Obviously, this effort took a lot of time and hard work, but the results will be very valuable." Surprisingly, only one faculty member (from the MSCD Philosophy Department) was adamant in his belief that the Library was not doing the best thing for the campus.

INFORMATION DELIVERY/INTERLIBRARY LOAN PROGRAMS

As described earlier, a critical component of the Collection Philosophy is an information delivery program that provides high quality and timely access to the resources not owned by the Library. In fiscal year 1994/95, a total of 10,894 items were requested to be borrowed (2,893 book and 6,391 articles). To meet user needs and expectations, an ongoing effort to strengthen the ID/ILL program continued at the same time Collection Development Services was developing the Philosophy and completing the journal review process. This effort included the following components.

Staffing. As indicated earlier, collection development and information delivery were designated as the first priority in the library-wide strategic planning process. This allowed two positions to be re-allocated to the Information Delivery/ILL Department. The first of these was a professional program manager, reporting to the Coordinator of Collection Development Services, who is responsible for: (1) designing and implementing innovative information delivery services utilizing electronic access technologies; (2) providing direction and management of the resulting document delivery service and integrating it with the ongoing ILL unit; (3) working with bibliographers to develop collection development strategies which result in the best utilization of resources; (4) representing the Auraria Library in a leadership role in local, state, regional and national activities related to ILL and emerging document delivery activities; and (5) working with all library service areas to keep them informed and participating in emerging document delivery/ILL programs.

The second position, a paraprofessional Library Technician I, was reassigned from responsibilities which were less of a priority in the organization. The ID/ILL student hourly budget was also sustained during a time when the overall library student hourly budget was reduced by approximately one third.

Automation. Streamlining the workflow in ID/ILL is very automation dependent. A major step was implementing (and continuing to implement) all possible features of the OCLC interlibrary loan system including bar code scanners, macros for identifying borrowing partners, IFM (Interlibrary Fee Management) and upgrading to the Windows environment. Also important to departmental efficiency is the use of an electronic management system, currently PRS. Other automation currently utilized includes Ariel (with plans to improve scanner quality and speed) and two telefax machines (with ongoing needs to improve quality and speed).

Electronic Ordering. Auraria had been an early developer of an electronic ordering mechanism for ID/ILL requests using campus e-mail capabilities. This service was greatly improved by participating in the *ZAP* project, a Colorado library e-mail request system that was developed by Colorado State University Library with funding from the Library Services and Construction Act (LSCA) administered by the Colorado State Library. The use of *ZAP*, with its direct interface to OCLC, significantly improves staff efficiency and user satisfaction.

An average of over 300 requests per month are received from campus constituents using *ZAP*. The use continues to increase due to effective promotion of the service by ID/ILL, the bibliographers, and other service points in the Library.

Commercial Document Delivery. In addition to the Auraria-CU Boulder Libraries Expedited Article Delivery Project (which supplies approximately 40% of journal article requests), the ID/ILL Department uses commercial document delivery services to provide timely access to journal articles. If an article cannot be supplied from CU-Boulder, the next step is *UnCover*. *UnCover* was chosen as the primary commercial document supplier as a result of the system-wide study of commercial document suppliers mentioned earlier.[15] If the charge per article is $12.50 or less, ordering is automatic. Approximately 25% of journal article requests are filled by *UnCover,* resulting in greater staff efficiency and quick turnaround averaging in the 24/48-hour range. Other commercial document delivery companies have not provided such consistent and timely service.

Article Access. Since Auraria Library has never had an extensive collection of journals, users, especially faculty, have not been accustomed to browsing the collection as a primary means of access or current awareness. In discussions with science and social science faculty, remote access from the home or office to the appropriate *Current Contents* database emerged as the preferred method of access to current literature. The cost of providing this access is currently too great to be a viable consideration for the Library.

Alternatively, Auraria (through the Colorado Alliance of Research Libraries) has obtained site licenses for *UnCover Reveal* and the *Personal UnCover Navigator (PUN)*. Although not totally comparable to *Current Contents,* these do allow for remote access at a much more reasonable cost. In addition to *UnCover,* and as a substitute for journal ownership, subscriptions to *Current Mathematical Publications* and paper editions of *Current Contents* for chemistry and biology are paid for by the Library and delivered to the departments for routing to faculty.

Subsidized Photocopying. At the time of Auraria Library's journal cancellation project, UCD math faculty suggested–since the Library was canceling so many journals in math and depending heavily on the CU-Boulder journal collection–that the Library pay for photocopying done by faculty at the CU-Boulder libraries. Although this suggestion was only half-serious in nature, the Library took it under consideration. The result was the ALFRESCO Card (*A*uraria *L*ibrary *F*aculty *RES*earch *CO*py Card). The Information Delivery/ILL Department has purchased, using collection development funds, a supply of copy cards good at either all CU-Boulder libraries (140 pages per card) or the CU-Health Science Center library (100 pages per card) and is distributing them to faculty who so request. In one semester, 228 cards have been distributed. This expenditure of $2,160 has created enormous good will toward the Library on the part of the faculty. Assuming that each faculty member may have each requested at least four articles through ILL at a cost of $4,560 (using the $5 per article from the CU-Boulder Expedited Article Delivery Project) or $26,950 (using the $29.55 ARL/RLG cost figure), the price of the cards is well worth the staff time (both at Auraria and at the lending library) and copying costs saved.

Other Projects. Several other information delivery projects have been tried and more are planned. A pilot project offering unmediated use of *UnCover* was less than successful. Faculty in campus chemistry departments were given individual *UnCover* accounts of $150 each and faculty in campus physics departments were given single departmental accounts, based upon $150 for each faculty member. The faculty were encouraged to order articles from *UnCover* and have them delivered directly to personal or departmental fax machines. Of the 39 faculty involved, only one (in physics) took regular advantage of the account to supply needed articles. Surprisingly, other faculty continued *ZAP*-ing requests to the ID/ILL Department for fulfillment.

CONCLUSION

Efforts to strengthen the relationship between bibliographers and information delivery/ILL continue. The Manager of ID/ILL programs regularly attends bibliographers meetings to provide input into collection development decisions. Statistical information regarding the number of journal articles requested from ID/ILL, and the associated cost, provides excellent management information to be used in deciding on new subscriptions. Likewise, statistical information on the use of the owned journal collection (kept by the Periodicals Desk personnel) and the projected costs of obtaining access through ID/ILL provides a rational basis for future collection adjustments (cancellations). Analysis of monographic circulation statistics and ID/ILL book borrowing statistics will provide similar guidance in book selection.

Other opportunities to expand the quality and timeliness of information delivery programs are also being explored. Several new unmediated projects are being discussed, possibly using *UnCover SUMO (Subsidized UnMediated Ordering).* The Colorado Alliance of Research Libraries is investigating a program which would, in effect, expand the Auraria-CU Boulder Libraries Expedited Article Delivery Project to include all Alliance libraries. Full-text databases are being tested and evaluated as another mechanism for providing information resources to library users.

The Auraria Library's commitment to cost-effective expenditure of the materials budget must be carefully balanced with the changing information needs and service expectations of the Library's user community. The ultimate goal of utilizing extremely limited fiscal support to satisfy the curricular and research information needs of students and faculty will require a fluid collection-building organization, close communication with reference and instruction personnel, and constant awareness of new and improved products and services. Auraria Library is committed and challenged to remain in the forefront of this swiftly developing field.

REFERENCES

1. Colorado Commission on Higher Education, *Approved Postsecondary Degree and Certificate Programs in Colorado Public Colleges and Universities, 1994-95* (Colorado Department of Education: Denver, 1994).

2. Keith Lance, *Statistics and Input-Output Measures for Colorado Academic Libraries* (Colorado State Library, Library Research Service: Denver, 1995).

3. Librarians per 1,000 FTE students–1.1; other staff per 1,000 FTE students–4.4; volumes per FTE student–22; serials subscriptions per 1,000 FTE students–149.

4. Jay Schafer and Camila Alire, "Changing a Library Services Faculty Model: The Major & Minor (M&M) Approach," in Richard AmRhein, editor, *Continuity & Transformation: The Promise of Confluence.* Proceedings of the Seventh National Conference of the Association of College and Research Libraries, Pittsburgh, March 29-April, 1995 (Association of College and Research Libraries: Chicago, 1995):131-137.

5. Colorado Central Library System, "Interlibrary Loan Study for University of Colorado Libraries: Auraria, Boulder, Colorado Springs, Health Sciences Center" (Wheat Ridge, CO: CCLS, 1992).

6. Glenda A. Thornton and Yem Fong, "Exploring Document Delivery Options," *Technical Services Quarterly* 12, no. 2 (1994):1-12.

7. Thornton & Fong, "Exploring Document Delivery," p. 11.

8. Carolyn Dusenbury and William Post, "Subscribing to a Research Collection." in *Acquisitions '91 Conference on Acquisitions, Budgets, and Collections held in Minneapolis, Minnesota, April 10-11, 1991*. Edited by D.C. Genaway, (Canfield, OH; Genaway & Associates, 1991), 67-80.

9. Mary Ann Chappell, "Meeting Undergraduate Literature Needs with ILL/Document Delivery," *Serials Review,* 20, no. 1 (1993):81-86, 94.

10. William A. Britten and Judith D. Webster, "Comparing Characteristics of Highly Circulated Titles for Demand-Driven Collection Development," *College & Research Libraries,* 53, no. 3 (1992):239-248.

11. Glenda A. Thornton, *An Examination of the Relationship Between Published Book Reviews and the Circulation of Books at an Academic Library,* 1993. Unpublished Ph.D. Dissertation, University of North Texas, Denton, TX, p. 43.

12. Charles A. Hamaker, "Some Measure of Cost Effectiveness in Library Collections, *Journal of Library Administration,* 16, no. 3 (1992):57-69.

13. Marilyn M. Roche, *ARL/RLG Interlibrary Loan Cost Study,* (Washington, D.C., Association of Research Libraries, 1993). p. iv.

14. "Ownership versus Access and Low-Use Periodical Titles," *Library Resources and Technical Services,* 39, no. 1 (January 1995):43-52.

15. Thornton & Fong, "Exploring Document Delivery," p. 11.

The Coming of Full-Service Access

Sue Samson

SUMMARY. This paper provides criteria for document delivery vendor selection and substantive data to support an innovative realignment of budget allocations, staffing, and services to better meet the expectations and needs of the academic library user. A review of two projects incorporating document delivery into ready reference and acquisitions is followed by an extensive analysis of four major document delivery vendors as part of a research project funded by The University of Montana Faculty Grant Program and the Mansfield Library. Criteria to assess four commercial document delivery vendors are analyzed based on their use by faculty representing three academic departments. The findings of all three projects support the integration of document delivery services within a framework of integrated collection development, technical services and public services. *[Article copies available for a fee from The Haworth Document Delivery Service: 1-800-342-9678. E-mail address: getinfo@haworthpressinc.com]*

INTRODUCTION

Opportunities abound and capabilities are evolving daily to provide unlimited horizons in which libraries can offer new and expanded services to an ever-growing demand for documents and full-service delivery. The first wave of electronic databases provided unprecedented access to information. This wave of access has been followed by an

Sue Samson is Assistant Professor, Humanities Librarian, and Library Instruction Coordinator, Mansfield Library, The University of Montana, Missoula, MT 59812-1195 (E-mail: ss@selway.umt.edu).

[Haworth co-indexing entry note]: "The Coming of Full-Service Access." Samson, Sue. Co-published simultaneously in *The Reference Librarian* (The Haworth Press, Inc.) No. 63, 1999, pp. 41-53; and: *Document Delivery Services:Contrasting Views* (ed: Robin Kinder) The Haworth Press, Inc., 1999, pp. 41-53. Single or multiple copies of this article are available for a fee from The Haworth Document Delivery Service [1-800-342-9678, 9:00 a.m. - 5:00 p.m. (EST). E-mail address: getinfo@haworthpressinc. com].

41

ever-growing expectation and demand for instant retrieval of complete copies of documents (Fitzsimmons 1996). Even more compelling is that the capability exists to fulfill these expectations and demands with new electronic services that merge libraries, education, and business within the larger information industry (Mosher 1995, Stockton and Whittaker 1995).

Innovative projects combined with innovative funding and partnerships must be piloted to test these new areas of service. At The University of Montana Mansfield Library, three pilot projects have been underway to explore new models of information retrieval, collection development, and serials access. Document delivery was implemented as a ready reference service in support of undergraduate research. Second, academic departments were able to use a portion of their library acquisition funding for document delivery beginning with the 1995/96 academic year. Third, a grant was received for the 1996/97 academic year to evaluate document delivery vendors as an alternative resource for serials acquisitions.

This paper provides a review of the two initial projects and an extensive analysis of four major document delivery vendors as part of the research funded by The University of Montana Faculty grant program and by the Mansfield Library.

BACKGROUND

Beginning spring semester 1994, three new processes were implemented simultaneously. First, three full-text databases–IAC Expanded Academic Index, IAC Business Index, and Newsbank–were incorporated into LaserNet, the electronic database network. Second, all undergraduate patrons with interlibrary loan requests were referred to the reference desk. Third, document delivery access to The UnCover Company (UnCover) was implemented as a ready reference service.

The three full-text databases provided a sound base of inter-disciplinary access to academic periodical literature and current event information. Full-text availability increased the library's current periodical holdings by 463 titles and newspaper holdings by 79 newspapers and 6 wire services. Currently, newspaper access has expanded to include 500 titles. These databases operate as a part of the electronic database network on 30 stations throughout the library. The IAC databases are also available through remote access.

Undergraduate referrals to the reference desk combined with mediated document delivery as a reference service provides a successful example of the use of technology to provide a new method of information delivery in a cost-effective manner (Samson and Brown 1996). The benefits to our library have been threefold. First, undergraduate patron interlibrary loan requests for periodical literature have been significantly reduced by this service, dropping from 21% of all interlibrary loan requests received in fiscal year 1993 to 11% in fiscal year 1995. As a result, interlibrary loan personnel are able to focus their services on graduate students and faculty, the original user group for this service.

Second, undergraduate reference service has a value added dimension. Because of the referral from interlibrary loan, students who might not previously have requested reference assistance are now able to receive direct support for their assignments. In addition, periodical holdings can be supplemented in a prompt, individualized method to students who frequently are working on short assignment deadlines (Waltner 1997).

Third, new and innovative technological access to information has been successfully incorporated into everyday reference service. Without increasing staff, a cost-effective reference service has been implemented by changing to a new model of information access. As librarians and students have become comfortable with the process, the service has proven more and more successful.

Mansfield Library is also exploring document delivery as part of collection development to improve access to current journal literature. Based on a formula, academic departments at The University of Montana receive annual allocations for library monograph acquisitions. Beginning with the academic year 1995/96, departments were able to use a portion of their annual acquisition funds for the purchase of journal documents using UnCover, the vendor chosen for this program. Five departments participated, requesting a total of 196 articles from 123 separate journals. Expenditures for the documents totaled $2,634.00. Subscription costs for these same titles would have been $67,500 for one year, establishing cost savings of 96.1%. These same departments were anxious to continue this access for another year and further expansion of this model is being explored in conjunction with a current serials cut of 12%.

DOCUMENT DELIVERY VENDORS:
ARE THEY READY OR NOT?

Information access is essential to academic faculty for both teaching and research. Faced with limited funding, the Montana Commissioner of Higher Education recommended that new technologies be utilized as a way of reallocating monies and redefining processes (Crofts, pers. comm.). An alliance between the library and commercial document delivery services offers the potential to accomplish these goals (Jaramillo and Lamborn 1996). A review of the literature revealed several evaluative studies of document delivery services (Truesdell 1994, Walters 1995, Mancini 1996), particularly as a comparison to interlibrary loan services (Kurosman and Durniak 1994, Jackson 1995, Waltner 1997). In fact, Kohl (1995) reports that The University of Cincinnati reduced annual journal costs by a net $180,000 while providing access to a much larger segment of academic journal publishing through CARL document delivery. None of these studies, however, evaluate the major document delivery services currently available to provide comparative data necessary to establish a standard set of criteria for expanding a new paradigm in the field of information management (Hong and Wang 1997, Marcinko 1997).

The state-of-the-art electronic databases network at The University of Montana Mansfield Library has provided our faculty and students with an increasing awareness of the universe of journal articles. Our currently configured network was accessed 36,542 times during autumn semester 1993 and 52,084 times during autumn semester 1994, an increase of 70.1% in one year. During the same time, interlibrary loan transactions also increased from 11,874 during autumn semester 1993 to 13,181 during autumn semester 1994, an increase of 11.0%. This period of growth in user access came at a time when a combination of budget restrictions and escalating serial subscription costs had required a freeze on the purchase of new journals with a serials cut expected. These data reflect trends at academic libraries nationwide. Thus, an exploration of a new paradigm of information access and retrieval was designed using faculty to serve as a model for analysis.

Objectives

This study establishes comparative criteria for document delivery services in order to evaluate their use as a mechanism to reduce the reliance on the traditional print journal subscriptions. Specifically, it was designed to: (1) create a profile of four major commercial document delivery services using standard criteria and establish their applicability to three focus areas–humanities, sciences, and social sciences; (2) assess the use of these services by faculty from the three focus areas using standard criteria; (3) determine the level of satisfaction by faculty to this method of access; and (4) evaluate the appropriateness of document delivery as an alternative or supplemental model of serial collection development.

Methodology

Three academic departments–English, Geology, and Management–representing humanities, sciences, and social sciences, were selected to participate in document delivery consumer trials. Four major document delivery services–EBSCOdoc, Faxon Finder, FirstSearch, and UnCover–were analyzed using specific criteria to determine two document delivery services for use by each department.

The participating departments were allocated $2,000 for each delivery service to be used for accessing journal literature. Thus, faculty in each department could access each of two services to an amount not to exceed $2,000 per service, a departmental total of $4,000. The project leader provided training as needed to initiate the trials and assistance throughout the trial period. Document delivery accounts were available from July 1 to December 31, 1996.

At the end of the trial period, surveys were distributed to departmental faculty to evaluate each document delivery service as a consumer product. A scale of 1-5 was used to measure the response of each participating departmental faculty member.

Results

A profile of the commercial services provided the basic selection criteria to determine which services should be used by each department (Table 1). These criteria must be reviewed frequently since vendors constantly change their interfaces, contents, and services. Three of the vendors–EBSCOdoc, Faxon Finder, and UnCover–have similar services and provide direct comparison. Essentially, an account with one of these services requires an annual fee which provides access to

TABLE 1. Profile of commercial document delivery services. Information provided by direct contact with the companies.

	Commercial Document Delivery Services			
Criteria	EBSCOdoc	Faxon Finder	FirstSearch	UnCoverWeb
Annual fee	$900	$1,050	$5,500	$900
Cost per document + copyright	$13.50 (50p)	$11.00 (20p)	$2.75	$6.50
Years of coverage	Variable	1990-	Variable	1989-[1]
Table of Contents service	$3.50/unit	NA	NA	free
Individual Profile Services	$35.00/profile	$2.00/profile	Alert	$20/profile
Number of titles	28,000	11,500	13,374	17,000
Humanities titles	<20% & soc sci[2]	18%	14%	9%
Science titles	70%[2]	55%	61%	51%
Social Science titles	<20% & hum[2]	23%	25%	40%

[1]UnCover Complete provides documents prior to 1989.
[2]Personal communication with vendor.

their collection of periodical articles. UnCover is unique in providing complete access to its database free of charge; an account provides a lower fee per article requested. Access to complete citations from EBSCOdoc and Faxon Finder requires an account. All three can be searched by name or title keywords. However, none are designed to be searchable databases similar to databases provided by companies such as IAC, SilverPlatter, or Wilson. These document delivery vendors focus their service on providing prompt delivery of documents–not on searching for information. Table of contents access is available free from UnCover and at a cost from EBSCOdoc. Individual search profiles of particular periodical tables of contents and word searches are also provided at additional cost from all four vendors.

FirstSearch has a unique structure. It provides access to a wide range of databases that are designed to provide access to information. Document delivery services are linked to its databases to provide direct ordering. For example, after a search is completed in a First-Search database, supply information is provided for each article and the user can order from a variety of document delivery services. It is necessary to have an account with this service as well.

The main criteria used in the selection process was the percentage of coverage of relevant journal titles to each focus area. Accounts with Faxon Finder and FirstSearch were established for English, EBSCO-doc and Faxon Finder for Geology, and FirstSearch and UnCover for Management. Access to these accounts was made available from July 1 to December 31, 1996.

Table 2 tabulates use of the four document delivery services by each department. UnCover received the most use of any of the services; 116 articles were ordered from 53 periodicals. It was also used by the most participatory department; 20.7% of the Management faculty used the service. However, First Search received no use by either the English or Management departments. Its unique structure and the need for addi-tional accounts with document delivery vendors made its use more complex. Further analysis of faculty responses at the end of the con-sumer trial provide additional information on its lack of use. EBSCO-doc was used to access 84 articles from 48 journals and Faxon Finder for 17 articles from 10 journals. Significantly, cost savings for docu-ment delivery versus comparable subscriptions ranged from 43.4% for the receipt of 3 articles from Faxon Finder to 95.0% for the delivery of 98 articles from EBSCOdoc. Total costs savings for all articles from all vendors were 93.8% over comparable subscriptions.

Use of the vendors provided a means of comparing both fill rates (Table 3) and costs (Table 4). EBSCOdoc provided the highest fill rate at 97.6% and the highest cost per article at an average of $18.76 per article. Fill rates for Faxon Finder (88.2%) and UnCover (87.1%) were similar as were their average costs per article at $15.73 and $15.79.

To determine the level of satisfaction of the faculty to this model of periodical access, surveys were distributed at the end of the trial peri-od to all faculty eligible to participate. Response to the survey in-cluded 25.0% of English department faculty, 56.3% of Geology facul-ty, and 62.1% of Management faculty. The primary purpose faculty cited for using document delivery during the trial period was for academic research, followed by teaching and academic development; personal interest was selected least often (Table 5). For those faculty who did not participate in the trial, lack of time was selected most frequently as the reason; lack of proper equipment was the next most common reason; and no interest or need and a preference for paper indexes were selected least often.

Participating faculty were asked to assess six specific criteria to analyze each document delivery service (Table 6). Comparing all cri-

TABLE 2. Use of four document delivery services by faculty from three academic departments, July 1 to December 31, 1997.

Criteria	English Department		Geology Department		Management Dept	
Number of Total Faculty	40		16		29	
Number of Participating Faculty	1 (2.5%)		5 (31.3%)		6 (20.7%)	
Vendor Selected for Departments	Faxon Finder	First Search	EBSCOdoc	Faxon Finder	FirstSearch	UnCover
Number of Articles	3	0	84	14	0	116
Number of Journals	3	0	48	7	0	53
Document Delivery Costs	$17.00	$0.00	$1,575.70	$219.00	$0.00	$1,607.75
Subscription Costs	$30.00		$27,498.00	$8,605.00		$19,114.67
Cost Savings	43.4%		94.3%	97.5%		91.6%

TABLE 3. Fill rates of commercial document delivery vendors used by faculty July 1 to December 31, 1997.

Vendor	Documents Ordered	Documents Received	Unfilled Requests	Fill Rate
EBSCOdoc	83	81	2	97.6%
EconFinder	17	15	2	88.2%
UnCover	116	101	15	87.1%
Total	216	197	19	91.2%

TABLE 4. Article and subscription costs of commercial document delivery vendors.

	EBSCOdoc	Faxon Finder	UnCover
Average	$18.76	$15.73	$15.79
High	$49.50	$18.00	$23.50
Low	$11.20	$13.00	$8.50
Annual Subscription	$900.00	$1,050.00	$900.00

TABLE 5. Analysis of purposes of faculty use of document delivery. Median value presented where 1 is low and 5 is high; number of respondents in parentheses ( ).

	Academic Departments			
	English	Geology	Management	Total
Academic research	5 (1)	5 (5)	4 (8)	5 (14)
Teaching and curriculum	2 (1)	4 (5)	3.5 (8)	4 (14)
Academic development	4 (1)	4.5 (4)	4 (7)	4 (12)
Personal interest	5 (1)	2 (3)	3 (5)	3 (9)

teria, UnCover received the highest ranking in each criteria. Of the 6 criteria, UnCover received a median value of 5, 4.5, and 4 in each of two criteria. EBSCOdoc and FirstSearch received similar series of rankings although FirstSearch was not ranked for two of the criteria. The unique configuration of FirstSearch provides access to numerous databases, some of which are linked to document delivery vendors.

TABLE 6. Analysis of commercial document delivery vendors used by faculty, July 1 to December 31,1996. Median value presented where 1 is low and 5 is high; number of respondents in ( ).

Criteria	Document Delivery Vendors			
	EBSCODoc	Faxon Finder	First Search	UnCover
Ease of computer interface	3 (4)	1.5 (4)	3.5 (6)	4.5 (8)
Success of searches	3 (4)	1.5 (4)	3.5 (6)	4 (7)
Adequate training	3 (3)	3 (3)	4 (6)	4.5 (8)
Speed of delivery of articles	4 (4)	4 (2)	NA	5 (7)
Quality of articles	3.5 (4)	3 (2)	NA	4 (7)
Relevance of database to field	3.5 (4)	2 (4)	3.5 (6)	5 (7)

However, subscriptions to these vendors were not made available for the trial period. Thus, use of FirstSearch resulted in a standard interlibrary loan request, negating direct comparison with the three other vendors on two of the assessment criteria–speed of delivery of articles and quality of articles. Faxon Finder received the lowest rankings overall although it had the same ranking as EBSCOdoc for speed of delivery of articles and adequate training. Faxon Finder received a rank of 4 in one criteria, 3 in two criteria, 2 in 1 criteria, and 1.5 in 2 criteria.

To evaluate the appropriateness of document delivery as an alternative or supplemental model of serial collection development, faculty were asked to assess seven statements about periodical access and traditional subscriptions (Table 7). Faculty in all departments provided high median scores for the effectiveness of document delivery as a method of acquisition for periodical literature in support of teaching and research. Statements in support of electronic access, document delivery, speed of access and desktop access received median scores of 5. The use of faxed or e-mail articles and the acquisition of more expensive literature through document delivery received scores of 4. The lowest ranking was a 3 for the statement supporting the traditional model of periodical ownership.

CONCLUSIONS

Three major conclusions can be drawn from this study. First, dramatic savings were realized during the trial period with the use of

TABLE 7. Analysis of faculty response to survey requesting response to periodical access options.

Statements	English	Geology	Management	Total
	Departments			
Electronic access to periodical citations is an effective method of acquisition.	4 (1)	4.5 (4)	5 (7)	5 (12)
Access to databases and document delivery provide good support for teaching and research.	5 (1)	4.5 (2)	4.5 (8)	5 (11)
Speed of access to articles is beneficial to research and/or teaching needs.	4 (1)	5 (4)	4.5 (8)	5 (13)
Desktop access to articles is beneficial to research and/or teaching needs.	5 (1)	4 (4)	4.5 (8)	5 (13)
Faxed or e-mail articles are adequate for research and/or teaching needs.	4 (1)	2 (3)	4.5 (8)	4 (12)
Document delivery is a good alternative for periodicals that cost >$300/yr.	4 (1)	3 (3)	4 (7)	4 (11)
I prefer the traditional model of periodical.	2 (1)	3 (3)	1.5 (8)	3 (13)

document delivery over the purchase of traditional subscriptions (savings ranged from 43.4% to 97.5%). The savings aspect is further substantiated by the first two pilot projects implemented by Mansfield Library. During the four year implementation of the ready reference project, only two titles have been identified where the number of articles ordered exceeded the annual subscription costs. Overall savings in this project are 97.7%. Similarly, the use of acquisition funds by academic departments for document delivery provided a 96.1% cost savings over comparable subscriptions.

Second, the standard evaluation criteria established in this paper can be used as a base of information to dovetail document delivery services within a framework of integrated collection development, technical services and public services (Young 1994). Redefining the role of serials acquisitions and processing within the broader scope of serials access services provides the opportunity to realign budgets and staffing based on emerging technologies and user expectations. Cost savings could be reallocated to implement a rapid document delivery system designed to integrate reference, interlibrary loan, serials acquisition and processing, and collection development (Khalil 1993, Hewison et al. 1995, Ferguson 1996). Again, these findings are supported by the results of the previous two pilot projects which integrated document delivery into a value-added reference service for undergraduates and provided faculty with desktop access to journal literature.

Third, faculty are receptive and anxious to participate in an effective method of document delivery as an alternative or supplemental model of serial collection development (Zastrow 1996). Participating faculty strongly endorsed this model of access. Even those faculty who were unable to participate largely were limited by time or equipment rather than lack of interest in the project. Working directly with the faculty to set up the accounts and provide training brought about rewarding dialogue about new access to information. The most significant part of the project was collaboration with the faculty which is central to the mission of the academic library. Although criteria and assessment of vendors are critical to decision making, the value of faculty collaboration is the single most important aspect of this study. Faculty remain the primary user of the academic library both through their own research and teaching needs and as the motivators of student use of the library.

The results of this study provide a base of criteria for document delivery vendor selection and substantive data to support an innovative realignment of budget allocations, staffing, and services to better meet the expectations and needs of the academic library user.

REFERENCES

Crofts, Richard. Montana Commissioner of Higher Education, personal communication, September 1995.

Ferguson, Anthony W. "Document Delivery in the Electronic Age: Collection and Service Implications." *Journal of Library Administration* 22(1996):85-97.

Fitzsimmons, Joseph J. "Document Delivery for the 90's and Beyond." *Journal of Library Administration* 22(1996):111-123.

Hewison, Nancy S., Vicki J. Killion, and Suzanne M. Ward. "Commercial Document Delivery: The Academic Library's Perspective." *Journal of Library Administration* 21(1995):133-143.

Hong, Yan and Hongjie Wang. "Confronting the Challenge of Electronic Document Delivery: A Literature Review." *Journal of Interlibrary Loan, Document Delivery, and Information Supply* 7(1997):3-13.

Jackson, Mary. "Redesigning interlibrary loan and document delivery service." *Wilson Library Bulletin* 69(May 1995):68-71.

Jaramillo, George R. and Joan G. Lamborn. "Document Delivery in Times of Shrinking Budgets." *Resource Sharing and Information Networks* 11(1996):5-13.

Khalil, Mounir. "Document Delivery: A Better Option?" *Library Journal* 118(Feb 1, 1993):43-47.

Kohl, David F. "Revealing UnCover: Simple, Easy Article Delivery." *Online* 19(1995):52-60.

Kurosman, Kathleen and Barbara Durniak. "Document Delivery: A Comparison of Commerical Document Suppliers and Interlibrary Loan Services." *College and Research Libraries* 55(1994):129-139.

Mancini, Alice Duhon. "Evaluating Commerical Document Suppliers: Improving Access to Current Journal Literature." *College and Research Libraries* 57(Mar 1996):123-131.

Marcinko, Randall W. "Issues in Commercial Document Delivery." *Library Trends* 45(Winter 1997):531-550.

Mosher, Paul H. "Real Access as the Paradigm of the Nineties." *Journal of Library Administration* 21(1/2 1995):39-48.

Samson, Sue and Barry Brown. "New Model for Ready Reference Document Delivery." *PNLA Quarterly* 60(Summer 1996):11-13.

Stockton, Melissa and Martha Whittaker. "The Future of Document Delivery: A Vendor's Perspective." *Journal of Library Administration* 21(1/2 1995):169-181.

Truesdell, Cheryl B. "IS Access a Viable Alternative to Ownership? A Review of Access Performance. *Journal of Academic Librarianship* 20(1994): 200-206.

Walters, Sheila. "The Direct Doc Pilot Project at Arizona State." *Computers in Libraries* 15(1995):22-26.

Waltner, Robb. "EBSCODOC v. CARL UNCOVER: A Comparison of Document Delivery Services at the University of Evansville Libraries." *Journal of Interlibrary Loan, Document Delivery and Information Supply* 7(1997):21-29.

Young, Peter R. "Changing Information Access Economics: New Roles for Libraries and Librarians." *Information Technology and Libraries* 13(June 1994):102-114.

Zastrow, Jan. "The Inner Workings of a Document Delivery Pilot Project." *Computers in Libraries,* 16(1996):20-24.

Exploring Document Delivery: Two Pilot Projects

Joanne M. Goode
Heike Mitchell

SUMMARY. This paper describes two pilot document delivery projects undertaken recently at Miami University of Ohio. The first pilot was conducted in conjunction with the Mathematics/Statistics Department. The second pilot, which involves all of the Science Departments, is currently midway through the projected test period of two years. Both pilot projects were developed to introduce faculty to the delivery of electronic table of contents and document delivery services. Our customer profiles, which can generate either table of contents or matches on keywords or author names, and the delivery of the documents, have been provided in a mediated environment. Library staff design and input the profiles and order the documents. This has afforded us the opportunity to talk often with our customers and observe their reactions to the projects. As a result, the service has become an expansion of reference services. Although the primary goal of both projects initially was, and still is, to encourage faculty acceptance of such services as a replacement for selected journal subscriptions, the obvious value of the services, as current awareness tools, has added a new perspective to our expectations of how the current project will grow and develop. It also ties in very nicely with our overall initiative of rethinking our reference

---

Joanne M. Goode is Science Librarian at Brill Science Library, Miami University, Oxford, OH 45056 (E-mail: goodejm@muohio.edu). Heike Mitchell is Serials Librarian at King Library, Miami University, Oxford, OH 45056 (E-mail: mitchehr@muohio.edu).

Correspondence should be sent to the first author.

[Haworth co-indexing entry note]: "Exploring Document Delivery: Two Pilot Projects." Goode, Joanne M., and Heike Mitchell. Co-published simultaneously in *The Reference Librarian* (The Haworth Press, Inc.) No. 63, 1999, pp. 55-71; and: *Document Delivery Services: Contrasting Views* (ed: Robin Kinder) The Haworth Press, Inc., 1999, pp. 55-71. Single or multiple copies of this article are available for a fee from The Haworth Document Delivery Service [1-800-342-9678, 9:00 a.m. - 5:00 p.m. (EST). E-mail address: getinfo@haworthpressinc.com].

services and our efforts to reach more of our remote and infrequent customers. *[Article copies available for a fee from The Haworth Document Delivery Service: 1-800-342-9678. E-mail address: getinfo@haworthpressinc.com]*

INTRODUCTION

A number of papers have been published in the last two years describing the increasing use of document delivery services in academic settings from a variety of perspectives. Several of these papers describe pilot projects. For instance, Chrzastowski and Anthes have described a pilot project conducted in a chemistry library setting.[1] Sheila Walters has written about a pilot project at Arizona State which focuses, in particular, on user behavior.[2] Minna Sellers and Joan Beam presented a case study of a document delivery project at Colorado State University.[3] Jan Zastrow has written about a project conducted at a community college.[4] These pilot projects have one element in common. They have been undertaken in an unmediated environment. In an unmediated environment, identification and ordering of documents is done by the end user of the document. This paper will describe two pilot projects conducted in an entirely mediated environment. Electronic tables of contents (TOCs) and search strategy outputs are delivered to faculty desktops. Document orders are then sent to project staff who place the orders with the vendors. Interestingly, many of our findings, as reported later in this paper, parallel those described in the unmediated projects.

The two projects described in this paper were conducted at Miami University, which is a state supported institution located in southwestern Ohio. The main campus of Miami is located in Oxford, Ohio. Enrollment at the Oxford Campus is approximately 16,000 (about 14,400 undergraduates and 1,600 graduate students). Miami also has two regional campuses and a European center located in Luxembourg which brings total enrollment to about 20,000. The Miami University Libraries include four libraries on the Oxford Campus; King Library which is the central library, Brill Science Library and two branch libraries. There are also libraries located at each of the regional campuses.

Prior to these projects, faculty at our campuses had only limited exposure to commercial document delivery services. Miami's interlibrary loan (ILL) department uses commercial delivery services on occasion, but these uses are at the discretion of ILL staff and are not obvious to customers of the ILL service. The delivery of electronic Table of Contents was also a new concept to many of the project participants. Although the library provided access to the CARL Un-Cover database for approximately three years prior to the project startup, only a small number of faculty had set up a Table of Contents alert despite the fact that the service was free during most of that time period.

The primary purpose behind both of the pilot projects is to explore options for reducing our serials budget. The last major serials cancellation project had been done in 1992. Projections from our serials vendors, as well as actual invoice costs and percentage increases over the last four years, coupled with a static budget, have made it clear that we can't continue to support our serials collection, in their present configuration, much longer. However, this time, rather than approaching the cancellations with a percentage cut across disciplines, as had been done in the past, we looked for some new approaches. We want to avoid yet another serial cancellation based on the model of distributing lists of current titles and asking which ones could be eliminated.

Miami University's primary commitment is to excellence in undergraduate education and the library recognizes the need to support that commitment with its collections. We need to examine ideas that will allow us to protect the undergraduate collection, but at the same time support the research of our faculty and graduate students. Access to, instead of ownership of, selected journals seems to be an obvious approach to try.

Our immediate goals are to introduce our faculty to a new means of accessing the journal literature and to try to determine, with their assistance, if this means can replace ownership of selected journal titles. Although we were very clear from the beginning in our discussions with faculty about the purpose of the project, we decided to offer these services prior to any in-depth discussions about canceling serial subscriptions. Our hope remains that when those discussions begin in the 1997/1998 academic year, we will have provided our faculty with a new tool in their decision making process.

During the same time period that our pilot projects were being planned and implemented, the entire library staff–both librarians and support staff–have been involved in the planning and implementation of a new reference service model. Out of this initiative came a commitment to examine our services to one segment of our customer community, our remote users. We defined those users as customers in our Miami community, primarily faculty, who did not come to the library to use the collections and services. This could be because they accessed the library electronically or because they did not actually use the library much at all. Although our TOC/Document Delivery projects were not initially planned in conjunction with the new reference service model, the outcome of our projects ties in very well with the goals of the model and demonstrate one new way that we have found to effectively reach a number of our remote customers.

PILOT PROJECT I

Background

The first introduction of an electronic Table of Contents Service and Document Delivery was planned with the assistance and cooperation of the Mathematics and Statistics Department. This was a small, start-up project. The Mathematics/Statistics Department was selected for several reasons. We knew from informal discussions that there was interest among a number of the faculty in such services and a willingness to experiment with a trial project. We also knew that most of the faculty use electronic mail frequently and work comfortably in an electronic environment. A third factor was that the percentage of increase and the subscription costs for serials in mathematics are among the highest in the sciences. We were also aware that the visual clarity and quality of the documents provided was particularly important in the disciplines of mathematics and statistics due to the presence of mathematical text and figures. We felt that if we could meet the standards for the faculty in these two disciplines, then we could make some assumptions about acceptance in other disciplines. When the project was presented at a Mathematics/Statistics Department meeting, we were asked if what we really meant was "If we could please them, we could please anyone?" In fact, that is what we did mean or intended to find out!

The first project was designed quite differently from our second one. A list of mathematics/statistics journals, subscribed to by the MU Libraries and costing more than $1,000, was compiled. The titles were then matched against two additional sets of criteria. First they had to be journals used primarily by the faculty. Secondly, electronic tables of contents and document delivery had to be available. Three titles were excluded because they could not meet the last set of criteria. The end result was a set of eleven titles (Figure 1). Vendor selection resulted in Faxon Co., Inc. as the TOC provider. We elected to have the TOCs for each title delivered weekly to the project coordinator, who in turn redistributed them to participants in the Mathematics Department. Included in the subscription cost was the right for unlimited distribution of those TOCs within our institution. CISTI, the Canada Institute for Scientific and Technical Information, and MATHDOCS, a service of the American Mathematical Society, were selected as the document delivery vendors.

The Mathematics/Statistics Department at Miami University supports 55 faculty. The project was presented first to the department liaison and the chair who were very interested in supporting the project and a meeting was held with the department faculty to present the project. A list of the titles selected for the project was shared with the faculty. This list included the invoice payments for each title for the last three years as well as the percentage of dollar increase for each of the titles. It was noted that these costs did not include the additional costs of serials management, such as processing, binding, providing shelf space, and reshelving. The proposed pilot project and its intent were then described to the faculty. Although there was certainly some skepticism about the value of this type of service and whether or not it could meet their needs, there was a general agreement that the costs of maintaining the serial collection, as it exists now, had become prohibitive and that things had to change. The faculty were willing to try out a combination of TOCs and document delivery and agreed to contribute their time to the project and to provide us with feedback as the project progressed.

Since our approach to this first project was from the perspective of targeting high-cost, research-level journals, the project was designed so that each faculty member would receive TOCs for each of the eleven titles on the list. Because we were interested in simulating an actual environment where these titles would not be in the collection, we removed the current issues from the library shelves. Faculty could place document orders for any articles identified in the Table of Contents. We did not supply articles via document delivery from older issues of these journals. The issues that we removed from the shelves

FIGURE 1. Pilot Project I–Journals in Project

Journal Titles	Publisher	Subscription	Costs		
		1995	1994	1993	1992
Communications in Algebra	M. Dekker	$1,742.00	$1,554.00	$1,243.00	$1,139.00
Communications in Statistics	M. Dekker	$2,283.00	$2,017.00	$1,825.00	$1,759.00
Discrete Mathematics	North-Holland	$2,384.00	$2,272.00	$2,316.00	$1,798.00
Inventiones Mathematicae	Springer-Verlag	$2,325.00	$2,263.00	$2,404.00	$1,889.00
Journal of Algebra	Academic	$2,184.00	$1,747.00	$1,273.00	$1,128.00
Journal of Mathematical Analysis & Applications	Academic	$2,318.00	$2,015.00	$1,680.00	$1,481.00
Journal of Pure & Applied Algebra	North-Holland	$1,554.00	$1,350.00	$1,417.00	$1,085.00
Mathematische Annalen	J. Springer	$2,114.00	$2,016.00	$2,047.00	$1,680.00
Mathematische Zeitschrift	J. Springer	$1,874.00	$1,829.00	$1,847.00	$1,468.00
		*Communications in the Statistics contains three separate titles			

were available for graduate students or InterLibrary Loan requests although none of them were requested by either group during the pilot period.

Observations

The first TOCs were delivered beginning in September of 1995 and the project ran through April, 1996. The project began with forty-four faculty. Four asked to be dropped from the project. Although the time frame for the project was originally one year, we stopped the project somewhat prematurely because a decision was made to expand the project to all of the science departments and to switch to a different vendor. In May of 1996, the participants in the project were surveyed.

The primary dissatisfaction expressed in this survey and throughout the project was with the quality of the photocopies. Ironically, most of the documents had been ordered as photocopies, delivered via postal mail or courier service, yet there was still dissatisfaction with the quality of the photocopies. The turnaround time that we received from both vendors was excellent. Document delivery vendors place a lot of their emphasis on turnaround time. Even though our participants commented favorably on the quick turnaround time, it wasn't a strictly necessary part of the service for most of them. The other element of

FIGURE 1 (continued)

Dollar Increase	% Increase	Table of Contents		Document Delivery	
		Uncover	Faxon	CISTI	MATHDOC
$603.00	53%	Yes	Yes	Yes	Yes
$524.00	30%	Yes	Yes	Yes	Yes
$586.00	33%	Yes	Yes	Yes	Yes
$436.00	23%	Yes	Yes	Yes	Yes
$1,056.00	94%	Yes	Yes	Yes	Yes
$837.00	57%	Yes	Yes	Yes	Yes
$469.00	43%	Yes	Yes	Yes	Yes
$434.00	26%	Yes	Yes	Yes	Yes
$406.00	28%	Yes	Yes	Yes	Yes

the project that disappointed participants was the lack of abstracts. Several mentioned a reluctance to order articles based on a title.

Figure 2 shows the total number of articles ordered and compares the costs of providing document delivery for these titles with the costs of subscribing to the journals. The project provided data for two thirds of one year. Although it is by no means a real comparison of cost, it is interesting and provides some "food for thought". The project did not run long enough to provide enough data to make actual cancellation decisions, but we did meet our goal of introducing our faculty to a new means of accessing the literature. This first project set the stage for our next steps, and provided library staff with some valuable experience on which to build our next pilot project.

PILOT PROJECT II

Background

A task force was set up in the Spring of 1996 to plan and implement the second pilot project. This task force was comprised of four librarians: two from administration, one subject selector and our serials librarian. The subject selector served as project coordinator for both pilot projects. The project was initially presented to all of the subject

FIGURE 2. Pilot Project I–Cost Comparisons

Journal Titles	Publisher	Subscription	
		1995	1992
Communications in Algebra	M. Dekker	$1,742.00	$1,139.00
Communications in Statistics	M. Dekker	$2,283.00	$1,759.00
Simulation and Computation			
Stochastic Methods			
Theory and Methods			
Discrete Mathematics	North-Holland	$2,384.00	$1,798.00
Inventiones Mathematicae	Springer-Verlag	$2,325.00	$1,889.00
Journal of Algebra	Academic	$2,184.00	$1,128.00
Journal of Mathematical Analysis & Applications	Academic	$2,318.00	$1,481.00
Journal of Pure & Applied Algebra	North-Holland	$1,554.00	$1,085.00
Mathematische Annalen	J. Springer	$2,114.00	$1,680.00
Mathematische Zeitschrift	J. Springer	$1,874.00	$1,468.00
Totals/Averages		$18,778.00	$13,427.00

selectors in the system and a meeting was scheduled with the selectors of the departments who would be participating. Subject selectors were encouraged to promote the project in their departments and could elect to be as involved in the implementation of the project as they wished.

Faculty in all of the science departments as well as psychology, geography and anthropology were invited to participate in the project. A report of each department's serial collection indicating the actual invoice prices paid for each serial title over the last three years, as well as percentage of price increases, was compiled. This report, along with a letter from the Dean of the Libraries, was sent to each of the department chairs and liaisons. The letter outlined the current economic environment for serials subscriptions and proposed the project as possibly providing a piece of the solution. The letter specifically asked for volunteers from each department to try out a combination TOC/Document Delivery service.

CARL UnCover was selected as the vendor for both the TOC service and the primary document provider. CISTI was selected as the backup document provider. The project was designed to run from May

FIGURE 2 (continued)

Dollar Increase	% Increase	No of Orders	Individuals	Total Spent	Aver Cost
$603.00	53%	35	3	641.23	18.32
$524.00	30%				
		6	2	220	36.66
		18	2	458.51	25.48
$586.00	33%	1	1	19	19
$436.00	23%	4	1	68	17
$1,056.00	94%	12	2	274.98	22.92
$837.00	57%	20	3	396.17	19.8
$469.00	43%	15	2	310.51	20.7
$434.00	26%	10	4	215.11	21.51
$406.00	28%	0	0	0	0
	Average				Average
$5,351.00	43%	121	7	2603.51	22.38

of 1996 through May, 1998. We were asked to mediate all aspects of the service during the trial project. This mediation included the setup and maintenance of each participant's profiles as well as the ordering and delivery of all documents. Although the mediation aspect has increased the workload significantly for the Library, it provides a mechanism to monitor both the progress and the costs of the project very closely. It also affords us the opportunity to be in close contact with our participants, to keep the Library visible in the process, and to add value to the service by performing all of the initial setup and any maintenance on participants' profiles.

Each participant was asked to fill in a registration sheet. Up to 50 journal titles could be selected, including journals not in the collection. The sheet could also be used to list research areas and related keywords and author names. This information was then used to set up an individualized profile for each participant. The setup of the TOC portion of the service was fairly straightforward and, with some exceptions, was done by a student assistant. Any problematic titles identified by the student were forwarded to our serials librarian who was a member of the task force. The keyword and author search strategies were much more of a challenge. The search engine used by the CARL UnCover Co. and the lack of in-depth subject indexing and abstracts for most of the records in the database placed limitations on the sophistication of the searches. We were very careful to tell participants that we were not promising to capture all of the new research coming out in their research areas, but that we should be able to capture some of it. Not all participants elected to use this part of the service.

We also set up three databases to track the data regarding the project using a relational database software program. The main database contains all the journals requested in the project. We use this database to record information about each of these titles such as ownership, requestor, number of articles ordered per month from each title, and cost. It is also used to track comments regarding the quality of copies from that particular journal and other customer feedback. A second database contains information about each participant including profile numbers and passwords. A third database is used to track information about orders. A report of orders is received by ftp from the vendor each month and downloaded into the database. Any records for orders filled by our backup vendor or from ILL are manually entered by a student.

Despite the fact that our end product is still in paper format, we have tried to make our process as paperless as possible. Participants mark the articles they wish to order in the electronic TOCs or search alerts as they receive them and forward the e-mail to a special account at the library. A student then orders the articles from CARL by electronically cutting and pasting the document order number into CARL's system. The articles are faxed to an account at the library, checked for completeness and then delivered via campus mail.

During the first few months of the project participants could order documents from journals in the collection, as well as journals that we did not own. Our purpose was, once again, to simulate a real situation. We encouraged participants to select journals that they used regularly to make comparisons, particularly regarding the quality of the copy. Unfortunately, we were forced to stop accepting orders from titles we subscribed to after several months. The volume of orders we were beginning to receive made the cost of conducting the project with that option prohibitive. In hindsight, we should have put a cap on the number of articles that could have been ordered from journals we own.

That would have allowed those comparisons to be continued over a longer period of time.

The volume of orders that we received–1,503 articles as of March 31, 1997–was higher than we had anticipated. Providing the table of contents, or, as one of our participants put it, "dropping all these wonderful citations into my lap" most certainly was one of the main stimulants. In fact, another participant said, "Ironically, I am using the journal collection much more actively because of the project than I ever did before." We had 60 participants in the project. Sixty-five percent ordered one or more articles. Twenty-five percent ordered 81 percent of the articles. This percentage closely parallels the anticipated distribution, described by Walters, where 80 percent of the demand would be created by 20 percent of the users.[5]

Observations

The first year of our second pilot was completed in May of 1997. By listening to our participants through informal feedback and two survey instruments, we now have sufficient foundation to plan for the next phase. The first survey was done in October of 1996 in conjunction with the announcement that orders from journals owned would be discontinued. Figures 3-6 illustrate the results of the first survey. The second was sent in April, 1997 as the first year of the project came to a close. This second survey was designed a little differently because the primary issue we wanted to explore was an acceptable turnaround time for the delivery of the documents. The survey results confirmed our impression that same day or next day delivery was really not necessary for our customers. Twelve percent of our respondents said that the one-two day delivery turnaround was "always" important. Fifty-eight percent said that it was "sometimes" important, and 19 percent said that it was "never" important. Of the respondents who did not answer that the rapid turnaround was "always" important, 36 percent indicated 6-9 working days was acceptable, Twenty-eight percent said 4-6 work days, and 24 percent said 2-4 days. Similar findings were reported by Chrzastowski and Anthes in their pilot project study conducted during 1993-1994. They reported that in most cases (88 percent), users opted to use regular mail delivery (3-5) days. Only 12 percent of their participants wanted requests within 2 working days.[6] Gossen and Irving, in their study which examined the cost-effective-

FIGURE 3. Pilot Project II–First Survey

Satisfaction with Table of Contents

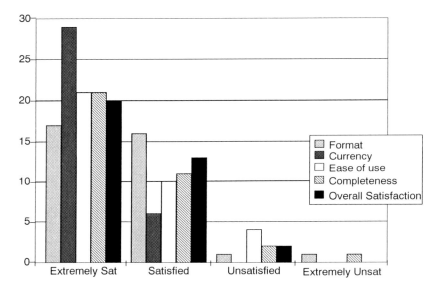

ness of canceling low-use journals, reported that 50 percent of faculty respondents indicated a delivery time of 3 to 7 days was acceptable.[7]

Long before the survey results were compiled, however, the obvious value of the project as a current awareness tool was emerging. Although customers were delighted and often quite surprised at the quick turnaround of document orders, the value of the Table of Contents delivery was the feedback. From both the open-ended sections of the surveys and informal feedback, some of the comments are very powerful indicators of the impact such a service can have. One participant, a chemistry professor, said "I am indeed most impressed with the profiles and tables of contents. They are of immense help to me, particularly since I am doing some polymer research where are our holdings are less extensive." From the Systems Analysis Department, a faculty member said, "I am catching up with my journal reading thanks to you." From another participant, "The Document delivery service and Carl UnCover are working wonderfully. For the first time in several years, I feel like I am keeping up with my field." And from a psychology professor, "I LOVE IT. It saves me time of having to run

FIGURE 4. Pilot Project II–First Survey

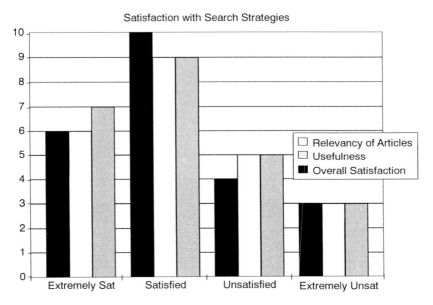

Satisfaction with Search Strategies

to the library, lets me know what of relevance to my research I need to read and provides this in a very timely fashion. This service puts a value on my time which I very much appreciate. This service will make opportunities for the faculty who use it." Figure 7 shows how components of the services were ranked in the second survey.

We continue to hear dissatisfaction with the lack of abstracts and some dissatisfaction with the quality of the faxed documents. All of the documents have been received via fax for the second pilot project.

Plans for the Future

Planning has begun for the next phase of this project. We are exploring options for expanding the project, possibly to two faculty groups beyond the science departments. As our plans develop, it is clear that the project may look very different with these new groups.

One option is the integration of the document delivery portion of the service into an established unit in the library which is better equipped to handle document delivery on an ongoing basis. In our discussions, we have explored the possibilities of integrating it into

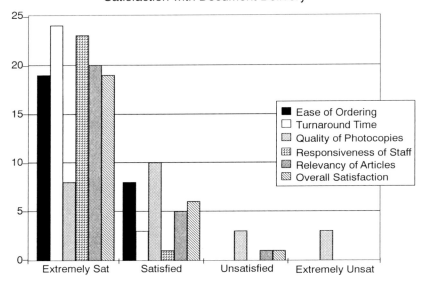

FIGURE 5. Pilot Project II–First Survey

Satisfaction with Document Delivery

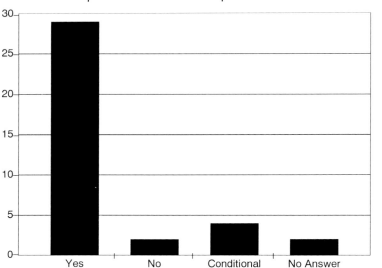

FIGURE 6. Pilot Project II–First Survey

Replacement for Ownership of Some Titles?

FIGURE 7. Pilot Project II–Second Survey

Which Aspects of the Service Are of Most Value?

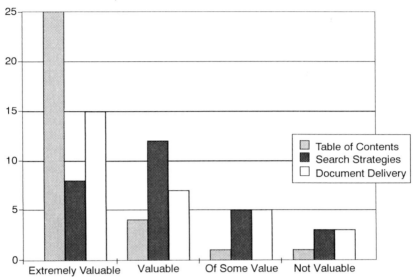

serials acquisitions or interlibrary loan. In the fall of 1997, we plan to experiment with routing document ordering for one of our new groups to the interlibrary loan department. We want to keep the design of the profiles and the interaction with the faculty within the domain of reference services and the responsibility of the subject specialists. In keeping with customer response regarding turnaround time, we want to explore a happy medium between the 2-3 week average turnaround now provided by the interlibrary loan department and same-day or next-day service currently being provided in the pilot project. We also need to keep the ordering process as convenient and quick as it is now and yet, at the same time, fit it into the work flow of the interlibrary loan department. The challenge is to maintain the dynamic, flexible nature of the service and to provide some stability and continuity for the document ordering process. Chrzastowski and Anthes' study examined that same issue, asking their users "Would you use this service if it was centralized at the main library?" They reported that "the response was split, with 19 "yes", 14 "no" and 2 "maybe" answers."[8]

Another option may be to offer only parts of the service to different groups. The reality of the costs of serials in non-science disciplines has to shape how we offer this service to faculty in those areas, if we are to realize any cost recovery. We have envisioned throughout our planning process to offer a TOC/Document Delivery service on a permanent basis would require funding with dollars recouped from serials cancellations. It may be that in departments where serials costs are not a significant part of the budget, we will offer electronic TOC services only.

In addition to adding different faculty groups and somewhat different types of services, we also plan to make some changes within our initial group of participants (numbering 62 as of May, 1996) in terms of how we are delivering our services. For instance, we would like to begin electronic delivery of documents to faculty desktops and/or to offer the option of faxing the articles directly to department fax machines. Several participants would like to revise their listing of journals or search strategies directly rather than have library staff perform that function; we may use a subset of this group to see how that might work.

We recognize that services such as the TOC/Document Delivery service described in this article are really interim measures and will outdate themselves with new technologies and publishing patterns that are already emerging. In fact, one extra benefit of this service is that it has helped us move some of our faculty into the realm of electronic informational services; this experience may help make the transition to the whole milieu of electronic journals somewhat easier.

CONCLUSIONS

With these projects, we have headed down a challenging road and, although we do not know precisely where the journey will take us, it promises to be an interesting one. What began as an experiment to find ways to reduce serial costs has evolved to an expansion of reference services and an enhancement of access services. This expansion has come at what we believe to be a bearable cost. Although we have not yet attempted to factor in staff and student time and other overhead costs into our estimates, the average per document cost, in the second pilot, has been $14.73 per article. Copyright charges have averaged out at $8.65 per document. The vendor fee for each profile is $14 annually (based on 100 profiles).

These projects have afforded interesting opportunities for librarians to become more aware of faculty interests and research projects, opening a few more doors to collaboration between the library and academic departments. The projects have helped move some of our faculty into the rapidly evolving world of electronic delivery of information services. We remain optimistic that the projects will also help our faculty and the library approach the realignment of our serials collection with new insights and tools.

NOTES

1. Tina E. Chrzastowski and Mary A. Anthes, "Seeking the 99% Chemistry Library: Extending the Serial Collection Through the Use of Decentralized Document Delivery," *Library Acquisitions: Practice & Theory* 19(2): 141:152.

2. Sheila A. Walters, "User Behavior in a Non-mediated Document Delivery Environment: the Direct Doc Pilot Project at Arizona State." *Computers in Libraries* 15 (October 1995), 22:26.

3. Minna Sellers and Joan Beam, "Subsidizing Unmediated Document Delivery: Current Models and a Case Study," *Journal of Academic Librarianship* 21 (November, 1995), 459:466.

4. Jan Zastrow, "The Inner Workings of a Document Delivery Project." *Computers in Libraries* 16 (October, 1996), 20:24.

5. Walters, 23.

6. Tina E. Chrzastowski and Mary A. Anthes, "Seeking the 99% Chemistry Library: Extending the Serial Collection Through the Use of Decentralized Document Delivery," *Library Acquisitions: Practice & Theory* 19(2): 144.

7. Eleanor A. Gossen and Suzanne Irving, "Ownership versus Access and Low-Use Periodical Titles." *Library Resources & Technical Services* 39 (January, 1995), 50.

8. Chrzastowski, 147.

Document Delivery in Academic Fee-Based Information Services

Suzanne M. Ward
Mary Dugan

SUMMARY. Academic libraries traditionally provide document delivery services to the campus-based community. Academic fee-based information services accept document requests from corporate, industrial, and professional clients who are willing to pay for a value-added service that includes rush handling, delivery to a third party, or locating an item with a vague citation. The Purdue University Libraries' Technical Information Service (TIS) has grown into a successful venture by developing staff with specialized skills to identify, locate, obtain, and distribute increasingly difficult document orders with short turnaround times. There are advantages to the parent academic library, especially the Interlibrary Loan (ILL) unit, in having a fee-based service to which time-consuming, unusual or expensive requests can be referred. With the potential to increase these advantages comes the need to define clearly the respective roles of these units. *[Article copies available for a fee from The Haworth Document Delivery Service: 1-800-342-9678. E-mail address: getinfo@haworthpressinc.com]*

Most academic libraries limit document delivery services, whether intracampus delivery of locally owned items or traditional interlibrary

Suzanne M. Ward is Head, Access Services, and Mary Dugan is Information Specialist, Technical Information Service, both at the Purdue University Libraries, West Lafayette, IN.

Address correspondence to: Suzanne M. Ward, Head, Access Service, Purdue University Libraries, 1533 Stewart Center, West Lafayette, IN 47907-1533 (E-Mail: ward@purdue.edu).

[Haworth co-indexing entry note]: "Document Delivery in Academic Fee-Based Information Services." Ward, Suzanne M., and Mary Dugan. Co-published simultaneously in *The Reference Librarian* (The Haworth Press, Inc.) No. 63, 1999, pp. 73-81; and: *Document Delivery Services: Contrasting Views* (ed: Robin Kinder) The Haworth Press, Inc., 1999, pp. 73-81. Single or multiple copies of this article are available for a fee from The Haworth Document Delivery Service [1-800-342-9678, 9:00 a.m. - 5:00 p.m. (EST). E-mail address: getinfo@haworthpressinc.com].

73

loan (ILL) services, to that group of people defined as the libraries' primary clientele. The primary clientele generally consists of people either enrolled or employed at the institution. Some libraries further restrict certain document delivery services to certain categories of patrons. Intracampus document delivery services might only be available for faculty, for example, or undergraduates might be excluded from ordering material through ILL.

Many academic libraries make no provision for obtaining materials for non-primary users. The reason for this exclusion is certainly understandable. Most academic libraries are hard-pressed to meet the document needs of their primary users in an efficient, cost-effective manner, without also taking on requests from potentially hundreds or thousands of alumni, citizens, or businesspeople throughout the state, region, country, or world. However, some academic libraries have looked for ways to serve these non-primary users without diminishing their ability to meet their primary obligation to the campus patrons. One effective solution for meeting this user need is to establish a cost recovery fee-based information service.

FEE-BASED INFORMATION SERVICES

A fee-based information service is a library unit that offers several services, usually document delivery and research, to non-primary users. The users are generally businesspeople, but also include entrepreneurs, consultants, corporate librarians, state agencies, trade associations, information brokers, commercial document suppliers, and medical or legal professionals. Services are offered on a cost recovery basis, although a few fee-based services strive to realize a profit. The unit is generally staffed by a combination of professional information specialists and support staff. With the possible exception of the manager or unit head, who may have a split assignment in another area of the library, the staff work exclusively for the service. A fee-based information service essentially offers on-demand corporate library services for companies too small to have their own library or for individuals who prefer to pay for professional research and document delivery services rather than spending the time to track down information or articles on their own. Although research services are an important, and often integral, component of a fee-based information service, this article focuses on document delivery. The authors' experience is with Purdue University's Technical Information Service (TIS), a fee-based service originally established in 1987 to meet the information needs of Indiana manufacturers. Over the years, TIS' mission has gradually changed. Although a high percentage of clients are still Indiana businesspeople, TIS serves people and firms all over the country and all over the world. Document delivery accounts for about three quarters of TIS' revenue. Most clients request photocopies of articles, patents, or other short documents, but TIS also lends books to clients with addresses in North America.

A SMALL BUSINESS IN A LIBRARY SETTING

A large part of TIS' success depends on its ability to respond quickly to document requests. For regular delivery, staff ship orders for locally owned materials the day after the request arrives. Orders for rush delivery are filled within a few hours. Corporate clients often have very short deadlines, and are willing to pay premium prices for just-in-time document delivery. They also have an ever-growing array of document suppliers from which to choose, so a fee-based service that cannot meet or beat the competition's turnaround times will experience a dwindling client list.

A rapid response is not the only key to an effective and successful fee-based service. Staff must also develop the expertise to:

- verify citations quickly and cost effectively
- ship materials to third parties
- use a variety of express shippers
- prepare international shipments
- provide accurate cost quotes
- track orders and provide status reports
- provide superlative customer service
- prepare accurate and timely invoices

A few fee-based information services choose to provide document delivery from their local collection only, but most also undertake to obtain items from other sources as well. For example, only about 75 to 80 percent of TIS' document requests can be satisfied by the Purdue University Libraries' collection. TIS chooses to fill the remaining 20 to 25 percent of client document requests by ordering them from outside suppliers.

GOING BEYOND THE LOCAL COLLECTION

Besides a consistently quick response to orders, another major factor in TIS' success has been the staff's expertise in quickly obtaining a wide variety of documents unavailable through traditional sources. Clients frequently order documents that are not held locally, and they are often willing to pay higher fees for the staff to obtain those documents on their behalf from other suppliers. Many of these orders are relatively routine, requiring a traditional OCLC search to identify libraries that hold the material, and then choosing potential vendors from fee-based information services affiliated with selected libraries. At TIS our first choice for document suppliers is other fee-based services, because our counterparts will:

- fill standard orders quickly
- meet clients' deadlines for rush orders
- notify us promptly if they cannot fill an order
- ship to third parties
- often reciprocate by ordering documents from us for their clients

At TIS we very rarely order material directly from another institution's interlibrary loan department. The regular turnaround time is generally not fast enough, and we also feel it is ethically questionable to request a free or low-cost copy for which we then charge our clients a fee.

Corporate clients request many specialized documents for which no holding library can be identified. Each service's manager decides whether it is cost-effective to continue searching for the material elsewhere. At Purdue's Technical Information Service, we continue the effort to meet clients' document needs. Some of the types of document suppliers we use are:

- publishers
- trade and professional associations
- document brokers who send runners to major libraries that have no fee-based services

- authors
- government agencies (local, state, regional, and federal)
- research centers
- commercial or quasi-commercial document suppliers that provide specialized materials (e.g., technical reports from NTIS or dissertations from UMI)

In an increasing number of cases, TIS clients request international documents. Although the requests usually include the name of the issuing agency, TIS staff have learned that it is much faster and more cost effective to deal with a single document supplier in each country or group of countries rather than to work directly with many individual foreign publishers, universities, or trade associations. For example, our European document broker is able to obtain a wide variety of papers, government reports, books, dissertations, conference proceedings, industry standards, and other material. We also use document suppliers in Japan, Australia, the United Kingdom, Canada, South Africa, and several other countries. The advantages of using these suppliers include:

- quick response
- the supplier's staff are knowledgeable about obtaining their country's specialized documents
- avoiding language barriers
- getting around time differences for phone calls
- avoiding lengthy negotiations to make shipping and pre-payment arrangements
- receiving one supplier's invoice for several items, rather than several invoices from several suppliers
- some suppliers bill in U.S. dollars
- possibility that the suppliers reciprocate when they need U.S. documents

DOCUMENT DELIVERY AND THE INTERNET

In a fee-based information service, the distinction between document delivery and research blurs as more publications become available, often exclusively, on the Internet. With increasing frequency, TIS staff access the Internet as part of the document identification and procurement process. We have identified three major uses of the Internet. First, several document vendors list their holdings on the Web and provide options for easily submitting online orders for specific items. CARL UnCover's journal listings and UMI's Dissertation Express sites are two examples. Second, many organizations list their publications on the Internet. By accessing the organization's Web site, TIS staff can quickly verify a document's existence, its price, and contact information for the supplier. Third, in a growing number of cases the document itself may be available more quickly from, or sometimes only from, a Web site.

This third category of Internet access to documents, often involving state or federal documents, is a mixed blessing. Sometimes clients have complete information about a report, but often they can only provide an incomplete or faulty citation, perhaps with only a subject and the name of the issuing agency. For these reasons, the Internet is usually not our first choice as a source for documents. However, sometimes it is the better source and sometimes the only source for these documents as more and more government agencies use the Internet to disseminate information quickly and cheaply.

A call to a state or federal department for either a known or an only vaguely identified document may yield any of these responses:

- the report is not yet available but information about it is included on the department's home page
- the department has all of its current reports listed in a keyword-searchable bibliography available through its home page, and the information included (such as report number) is necessary to order the document
- the document is out of print and a reprint is unlikely, but an electronic version is available on the Internet
- the report is available in print, but since it is out of date, the department prefers that users consult the updated Web version
- the report is *only* available on the Internet

Electronic document procurement via the Internet may provide instant access, but electronic access presents a number of challenges. Setbacks include messages that the Universal Resource Locator (URL) does not exist or that the server may be down. Having located the producing site's home page, the searcher may still spend a lot of time clicking through link after link to reach the required document.

Once the document is located, there can be further problems. For example, TIS recently received a request for a 500-page report only available on the Internet. The originating agency provided the exact Web address so we located it immediately. However, printing such a massive document crashed our local area network's server, requiring an emergency visit from the Libraries' computer support unit.

These examples of rapid, cost-effective, efficient, and professional document delivery from the local collection, from other U.S. collections and sources, from international sources, and from electronic sources demonstrate that document delivery in fee-based services must be as comprehensive, integrated, and seamless as possible. Corporate clients are willing to pay the costs (within reason) for just-in-time document delivery. Since these clients have many choices of fee-for-service organizations, an academic fee-based service must distinguish itself by its ability to identify, locate, obtain, and distribute increasingly difficult document orders with increasingly shorter turnaround times.

ADVANTAGE TO THE ACADEMIC COMMUNITY

The specialized skills that fee-based information service staff develop to meet the document needs of their corporate clients can be put to good use by the parent library. The Purdue Libraries have explored some of these options, but the possibility exists of extending the arrangement even further.

The Purdue Libraries Access Services Department consists of four units, two of which are Interlibrary Loan and the Technical Information Service. ILL staff routinely refer to the Technical Information Service the following types of document requests:

- from for-profit organizations
- from international addresses (except Canada)
- from individuals
- from institutions requiring rush delivery services, with the exception of those institutions with which the Purdue Libraries have reciprocal lending arrangements
- from local patrons for material that is unavailable through traditional ILL sources or from the limited number of other sources

ILL uses, e.g., military specifications or technical reports available only from the issuing organization

These requests either fall outside the scope of ILL services, or are specialized services for which the Purdue Libraries assess a fee. The fee-based service is staffed, organized, and experienced to identify, provide cost quotes, process any necessary pre-payments, fill, deliver, and bill these types of requests.

The ILL unit could further draw on TIS resources by calling on the staff's expertise to handle transactions such as:

- verifying citations in commercial databases
- obtaining documents available only from the issuing agency or from commercial suppliers that ILL does not use
- obtaining selected international documents
- expediting requests from local patrons for rush delivery
- identifying and downloading documents available only on the Internet or from full-text databases

Rather than developing similar skills in both the ILL and the fee-based service, the library could decide to eliminate the duplication and outsource the more unusual ILL requests to the fee-based service. The ILL staff would then be able to concentrate their efforts on the ever-growing numbers of relatively straightforward requests.

In making this decision, issues to consider include:

- Definition. Does a policy clearly describe what types of requests will be handled by each unit?
- Loss of expertise. Does the ILL staff lose the opportunity to develop the expertise of handling difficult requests?
- Identify the client. Does the fee-based service obtain items for the ILL unit, or for the individual patron?
- Fees and billing. Does the library reimburse the fee-based service at its published rates (typically the document cost plus a standard handling fee)? Or does the fee-based service handle these orders at a discount from its regular rates? If so, can it still cover its costs? If the transaction is one for which the patron would have paid, does the fee-based service bill the library, or does it bill the end user? If it bills the user, does it charge its regular rates, or a discounted rate? If it charges the patron the discounted rate, does the library make up the difference?

- Copyright. A fee-based service might pay copyright, or obtain material from a supplier who pays copyright, in cases where the ILL unit would have ordered it under the fair use provisions of the copyright law. Does the user category (campus patron or corporate customer) have a bearing on copyright? Who pays the copyright fees?
- The fee-based service's mission and capacity. A fee-based service's mission is generally to serve off-campus business professionals. Will handling these specialized requests from ILL diminish the ability to provide fast, responsive service to corporate clients? Or can the fee-based service expand to accommodate requests from both the internal and the external sources?
- Status reports. If a campus patron asks ILL staff for the status of a request which was referred to the fee-based service, can the question be answered quickly and accurately?
- Other library staff. Does the rest of the public services library staff understand how and why distinctions are made about which unit handles which kinds of requests? Do they refer patrons appropriately?

The main objective of any document delivery activity is to obtain the material quickly for the patron and at a reasonable cost. There are a number of ways that a library's fee-based information service can act as an outsourcing agent for its own institution's ILL department under certain clearly defined conditions. Thus the fee-based service staff draw on their specialized knowledge and document supplier network to fill some academic community's information needs, without diminishing their ability to meet the information needs of their own clientele.

Index